D1384331

# You Can Always Judge a Book by the Company It Keeps.

## Read What the Clients Are Saying About Tony Jeary—Mr. Presentation™

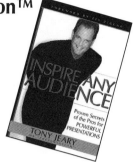

### *Speaking from the Top*
### *& Inspire Any Audience*

"I am convinced that, with your help and support, my team and I are now better able to communicate the value of our business with our associates, stockholders, and analysts."

**TOM GRIMM**
President & CEO, SAM's Club

"Your ability to speak well and give effective presentations is central to your success as an executive. This book shows you how to do it — better than before."

**BRIAN TRACY**
Brian Tracy International

"Inspiration is no small matter when communicating important initiatives to large, independent minded audiences like Ford dealers. I have found Tony Jeary's insights on inspiring audiences to be both helpful and practical."

**JIM O'CONNOR**
President, Ford Division, Ford Motor Company

"Speaking is a skill, which simply means it can be learned, particularly if you have the right teacher. Tony Jeary is the right teacher."

**ZIG ZIGLAR**
Zig Ziglar Corporation

"There is no more important skill than getting on your feet and inspiring an audience. Let Tony Jeary show you how."

**KEN BLANCHARD**
Author, *One Minute Manager*

"I would like to thank you for your role in supporting me personally as well as my staff in the area of presentations. You came to me with high recommendations; and now, as our relationship is approaching a year, I can truly see why you were so highly touted."

**J. RUSSELL REID**
President, InsureZone

"It is a pleasure to acknowledge Tony Jeary and his fantastic work as a first-rate business consultant and personal trainer. . . . He is a man with a deep well of skills and a treasure trove of abilities found only in those few who have persevered to achieve great success."

**DR. ROBERT H. SCHULLER**
Founder, *Hour of Power*

"Understanding the process that Tony has outlined in this book is essential to giving good talks."

**TOM SLONE**
Retired Senior Executive Vice President,
The Associates 1st Capital

"If this book gives you 10% of the confidence and enthusiasm in front of any group that Tony Jeary exhibits in front of all groups, it will be your best investment ever."

**JOE HANNAN, JR.**
Former President, Lambroghini, USA

"Your library of information, ideas and systems is a real treasure. And your one-on-one coaching is absolutely the best!"

**R. MORRIS SIMS**
Corporate Vice President, New York Life

"After spending an evening and ten hours the following day with you, I can say that I feel my money was well spent. I left Dallas confident that I had accomplished the goals I had set with you."

**MARK MAGNACCA**
President, Insight Development Group, Inc.

". . . the momentum of the knowledge and skills you've imparted spreads throughout Chrysler. Our satisfied customers and our very future will be truly enhanced because of your fine efforts."

**T.R. CUNNINGHAM**
Executive Vice President, DaimlerChrysler

"There in no question in my mind that your coaching will help my ability to connect with and to have more impact with my audiences."

**THOMAS R. PARISH**
Partner, Carlisle & Company, Inc.

"Tony Jeary's book *Speaking From The Top* is a textbook on how to master the skill of presenting. Whether you are in sales or the CEO of a billion-dollar corporation, let Mr. Presentation™ be your personal coach."

**MARK VICTOR HANSEN**
Best Selling Author, *Chicken Soup for the Soul* and authority on human potential

"Public speaking is a skill, an art form that has the power to move an audience into permanent change or action. Tony Jeary's book *Speaking From the Top* will help you master the art of speaking and maximize your ability to reach all your goals."

**JIM ROHN**
Author, *Five Major Pieces to the Life Puzzle* and *The Treasury of Quotes*

"A tremendous thought-provoking and entertaining book that will be a help to **EVERYONE**."

**CHARLES "TREMENDOUS" JONES**
Author, *Life Is Tremendous*

"*Inspire Any Audience* delivers! I encourage you to try the Jeary Theory—practical, effective steps make your presentations effective."

**JIM TUNNEY, ED.D, CSP**
CPAE Speaker Hall of Fame

"Presentation skills are key to leadership! *Inspire Any Audience* is packed with specific solutions to help your presentation hit the bull's eye. A must read for any leader to find the key to unlocking leadership potential."

**JOHN C. MAXWELL**
Founder, INJOY Ministries

"Tony Jeary has mastered the art of inspiring an audience. Anyone who wants to improve his or her platform skills with real, proven ideas and techniques needs this book. I recommend it without hesitation."

**PATRICK O'DOOLEY, CSP**
Former Board Member,
National Speakers Association

"Everybody knows that to reach the top these days, you have to acquire the ability to speak in public. *Inspire Any Audience* will help one learn the skill."

### TERRANCE J. McCANN
Executive Director, Toastmasters

"This is an outstanding book for anyone wishing to acquire extraordinary communication skills. Easy-to-read. Practical. Chock-full of tips and tactics you can put to use right away"

### NIDO R. QUBEIN, CSP, CPAE
Creative Services, Inc.

"To inspire is an intrinsic ongoing change vs. external motivation. This is an excellent manual for moving your presentation from successful to significant."

### NAOMI RHODE, CSP, CPAE
'97 Cavett Winner and Former President ,
National Speakers Association

"Tony's advice in this book is right on target for executives who increasingly don't have a second chance to make a first impression. The honeymoons for new CEOs are getting shorter and shorter, and those who don't use Tony's team approach in executive messaging are going to be at greater risk of premature retirement."

### GEORGE LOWE
President, Lowe & Associates

"In our SUCCESS Seminars, I get to see first-hand the power of words spoken by people who hold the highest position in their fields. *Speaking from the Top* reveals the keys to helping top executives maximize the impact of their presentations."

### PETER LOWE
Peter Lowe Success Seminars

"In the book *Inspire Any Audience*, Tony Jeary has given more great ideas on more varied subjects about presenting than any other author I have read. This is a very practical book, and at the same time it is fun to read. If you make presentations, you should have this book. I highly recommend it."

**JIM CATHCART, CSP, CPAE**
Former President, National Speakers Association
Co-Owner, Professional Speaking Institute

"Regardless of your own personality style, the key to good communication is being able to help your audience know exactly what you are trying to say to them. That is the essence of an effective communicator. Tony Jeary has mastered this art and can help you do the same."

**ROBERT ROHM**
Founder, Personality Insights

"*Inspire Any Audience* is an inspiration for anyone using its valuable content. An important confidence-building step for all presenters. "

**AL LUCIA**
President, ADL Associates

"I have had the opportunity to see many presenters and guest speakers with varied skill sets and expertise. I have seldom seen anyone keep the attention of an audience as you did at our leadership conference."

**PENNY HILER**
District Activities Coordinator, FTD Association

"*Inspire Any Audience* is a comprehensive and easy-to-read guide for anyone who wants to prepare and deliver top-notch presentations."

**TONY ALESSANDRA, PhD, CSP, CPAE**
Author, *Charisma and The Platinum Rule*

# SPEAKING FROM THE TOP

# SPEAKING FROM THE TOP

How the World's
Top Executives
Deliver Dynamic
Presentations
That Move People
and Markets

## TONY JEARY

MR. PRESENTATION™

THE PRESENTATION EXPERT

TO CONTACT Tony Jeary—Mr. Presentation™
CALL Dan Miller
Business Manager
800-982-2509

## DEDICATION

To the many friends, clients, associates, fellow authors, and gifted communicators who have taught me the most about the power of presentations:

Zig Ziglar, Robert Schuller, Brian Tracy, Ken Blanchard,
J. Russell Reid, James G. O'Connor, Robert Rohm,
George Lowe, Nancy Michaels, Peter Lowe,
Thomas R. Parish, R. Morris Sims, Mike Reeves,
T. R. Cunningham, Mark Magnacca, Ernest J. Parsons,
Joe Hannan, Jr., Greg Smith, Tom Grimm,
Mark Victor Hansen, Jim Rohn,
Charles "Tremendous" Jones, Chuck Goodrick,
John Maxwell, Patrick O'Dooley, Terrance J. McCann,
Naomi Rhode, Nido R. Qubein, Jim Cathcart,
Terry Washburn, Tony Alessandra, Buz Barlow,
Toby Slough, Eric Harvey,
Mark Pantak, Dottie Walters, Juanell Teague

# TABLE OF CONTENTS

# CONTENTS SUMMARY

## CHAPTER ONE:   The Executive Speech

All words spoken by all people are *not* equal. The words of top leaders have a powerful impact on people and organizations. When the leader of a business speaks, there is always a response of some kind from many sectors. The executive speech is the foremost vehicle for garnering a high level of support from all audiences—both internal and external.

## CHAPTER TWO:   The Team Concept

Using the team approach elevates the quality of a presentation. When executives deliver speeches, they are delivering total messages that include words, visual effects, audio effects, and an intangible aura that will either build up or detract from their images as leaders. The key is to bring in the right people for the presentation team at the right time for the right assignments for the right duration, being sure the functional categories are covered and that each role is filled by a person who has the necessary expertise, background, and desire to help.

Public speaking is one of the top fears of human
beings. Fear reveals itself in presentations as nervousness, poor voice tone/inflection, and negative body language. The right preparation team can build the
executive's confidence in practical and highly significant
ways. Knowing that one will be successful is the greatest confidence builder of all.

Every presentation should be built upon a foundation of
specific objectives, and the "funneling process" is a
unique vehicle to help the presenter build objectives.
There are essentially four types of messages: messages
of influence, messages of information and education,
messages of inspiration, and messages of an emergency or impromptu nature. Understanding the audience and moving audience members to the desired level
of response are critical to the success of the presenter.

The team approach ensures that the executive
always has the best possible information and that all
technological resources are maximized. A good presentation team helps the executive determine the
type of presentation to be made, identifies the audience types and expectations, and obtains vital information about the presentation venue. The 3-D
Outline™ provides a simple, quick means of identifying and quantifying a great deal of information in a
small amount of space.

The "funneling process" and the 3-D Outline™ are
excellent tools to help the executive and the presentation team identify clear, written objectives and create
the details of the presentation. The 3-D Outline™
identifies the time budgeted for each segment of the
presentation, displays a bullet list of the information
to be presented in each segment (the "what" dimension); establishes the reason each segment is presented (the "why" dimension); lists the technical
support and presentation tools that will be used (the
"how" dimension); and provides a transitional statement that will smoothly move the presentation to the
next segment.

**CHAPTER SEVEN: People** 99

Although most speechmakers readily acknowledge that they should consider the audience profile in preparing their speeches, an amazing number do not. The key to connecting with audience members is to thoroughly understand them. Recognizing audience "character" identities and personality types and meeting audience members prior to the presentation are critical to the success and impact of the speech.

**CHAPTER EIGHT: Places and Things** 115

With the help of the presentation team, the potential of each type of speaking venue can be maximized. The preparation and planning process is enhanced by the use of a facilities checklist and an equipment checklist. If the team diligently collects information about the venue and plans the use of equipment, there should be no facility or equipment-related surprises on the day of the event.

**CHAPTER NINE: Material** 131

To capture the emotions, a speech should contain material with which the audience can identify personally. Good stories certainly achieve this goal—stories that are about real people, involve real-world situations, have powerful endings with unique twists, and are positive in nature. Stories should be matched to the executive's objectives and should be compatible with the overall emotional tone of the message. Every top executive should build a private file of stories, quotes, and examples that can serve as a powerful arsenal of support for his or her presentations.

**CHAPTER TEN: Preparation and Practice** 143

Great presentations are always well rehearsed. Preparation promotes spontaneity. Practice and rehearsals, especially under the direction of a professional coach, can help identify the strengths and weaknesses of both the content and the delivery of the presentation. Dress rehearsals are a must for ensuring there are no surprises on the day of the event. The executive must know the material; be confident in his delivery; and make sure the slides, overheads, charts, and video clips will send the messages they are intended to send.

*Conclusion: Go Team Go!* 155

## ACKNOWLEDGEMENTS

Thanks to all who have participated in the effort to bring this book to life. Your input, feedback, and editorial support are what give the reader extraordinary value with this book.

Jay Heinlein, John Alberg, Kent Mazzia
Betsy Gibson, Tom Sloan, Chuck Goodrich
Al Lucia, Jim Cherfoli, Jan Dargatz
John Davis, Nell Miller, Nonie Jobe
Jim Norman, Jim McKenna

# THE PURPOSE
# OF THIS BOOK

*S*peaking from the Top breaks through the "unconscious incompetence" of executive speech patterns. Incorporating the methods and practices presented will lead to dramatically improved performance and greater impact with every presentation.

*Speaking from the Top* presents a team concept designed to streamline and improve presentation development for all executives. Dynamic leaders understand that every presentation must be on target, whether they are speaking to an internal or external audience. *Speaking from the Top* provides a methodology to insure that every executive speech hits the mark by sending the desired message and meeting the expectations of the audience.

Top business leaders face three major challenges in the preparation, development, and delivery of presentations:

**1) TIME:** Executives have many vital responsibilities and are so busy multitasking that they do not have time to adequately prepare presentations. They feel they must go it alone, or, at most, rely on a single speechwriter. Implementing the team concept of *Speaking from the Top* saves priceless time while dramatically upgrading the quality and impact of every presentation.

**2) EXPERTISE:** Top executives are a talented and brilliant lot, but few fully utilize the technical help and expertise that surround them. Executives utilizing the principles in *Speaking from the Top* leverage all available resources to improve the four key components of successful presentation planning:

- Effective information and statistics
- Graphics and multimedia concepts
- Technical support
- Presentation delivery

**3) PRESENTATION SKILLS:** Many executives lack the skills to deliver energetic, effective presentations. Along with a professional coach and dynamic team, *Speaking from the Top* guides the reader to continually improve speaking skills while increasing the effectiveness of every message.

## HERE'S MY GUARANTEE

f you and your team apply the principles discussed here, you will:

- Be better prepared (in less time)
- Be more confident
- Connect with your audience
- Present a message that sensibly links to other executives on the platform

Scores of executives and thousands of managers around the world have experienced the power of the approach we take in *Speaking from the Top*. The unique challenges that face top executives, along with the internal resources they have available, make dynamic presentations that move people and markets a reality.

# YOUR WORDS COUNT MORE

T HE SPOKEN MESSAGE OF AN EXECUTIVE reflects the heart and soul of a corporation. No speech or executive presentation is as important as the one that comes "from the top." For that simple reason, every corporate executive faces the challenge of creating and delivering speeches and presentations that are consistently dynamic and powerful. Corporate executives must clearly convey their key messages in the simplest manner possible, all the while portraying positive, reassuring images of themselves as they motivate their audience members to act or think in the ways they desire.

We live in a visual, fast-paced, streamlined world; and the most successful presentations use many dynamic tools to present concepts in concise, powerful, and readily understood ways. This book is written to help corporate leaders better understand and use these tools. The basic methods advocated in this book employ a team concept using detailed planning documents, coupled with principles for effective storytelling and presentation delivery.

When CEO's and other top executives don't reach their potential as excellent speakers and presenters, it is usually because they fail to use the many resources available to them. We love to hear tales about great speeches written in fifteen minutes on the backs of envelopes or napkins, but such stories are the exception rather than the rule. The best executive speeches and presentations are carefully crafted and presented in the most favorable environments possible. The words of top leaders to shareholders, boards of directors, employees, Wall Street analysts, and the general public shape the future of a business, and they deserve the best treatment.

I've been privileged to coach many top executives from some of America's foremost companies. All of these leaders were extremely intelligent people with great messages to share. Prior to our time together, however, most of them were unaware of the wide range of tools, techniques, and processes available to elevate their presentations from ordinary to extraordinary. My experiences with these leaders led me to write this book.

This is my eighth book dealing with presentation skills, but it is unique in its focus. The top executives of corporations have a special niche to fill. Their words often impact the lives of many thousands of people, and it is imperative that their messages be showcased and delivered in the most favorable and effective ways. Their inspiring and forward-moving directives *must* be clearly understood. After all, the direction of their business units, large and small, will depend on their audiences' interpretation of what they say. There is no room for ambivalence in an executive presentation. Every word must count. A "failure to communi-cate" can be not only costly, but also devastating to both the company's future and the executive's personal career.

Many corporate leaders fail to recognize the far-reaching impact of their words. When top leaders speak, their words are scrutinized closely. Their listeners consider not only WHAT is said but also HOW it is said—even when and where it is said! They use the spoken statement as a means of evaluating the believability of the speaker. The challenge for the executive? *Every* presentation must be thoroughly prepared and power-fully delivered. A leader can't run the risk of delivering anything less than a stellar presentation *every time out*.

In recent years, much has been written about the importance of corporate teamwork. One of the hallmarks of business train-ing and education for the past decade has been the need for involving employees from all levels of an organization in collec-tive efforts. I believe in teamwork as much as anyone and have taught the principles of teamwork to employees of some of America's largest companies. Having said this, I am also of the opinion that no team can ultimately do what a top executive does. No team can replace a corporate leader. The leader starts things rolling. The leader energizes the team and sustains the team's momentum. The leader is the point person. The leader's words give the team direction and focus.

Conversely, the team gives support and information to the leader. When it comes to speechmaking and executive presenta-tions, leaders need to learn how to *leverage* team principles as they create their speeches. They need to learn how and when to use a team to help them do what only they *can* do as leaders.

The potential contribution of a *preparation team* to an executive presentation is enormous. Let me tell you how to maximize that contribution.

# CHAPTER ONE

# THE EXECUTIVE SPEECH

I T MAY BE DEMOCRATIC TO THINK THAT the words spoken by all people are equal. In a theoretical sense, this may be true. In a practical sense, the words of leaders command more attention and are given more weight. In the business world, board chairpersons, CEO's, presidents, and senior executives of corporations are the leaders of commerce and the "captains of indus-try" who drive the economic engines of the world. These leaders have power and authority within specified spheres of influence, and their words carry the potential to dramatically transform the personal and professional lives of hundreds of thousands of people.

> When the leader of a business speaks, there is always a response of some kind.

When the leader of a business speaks, there is always a response—favorable or unfavorable, but nevertheless a response.

People listen to executive speeches with an ear for action. They expect to hear something that will provide information to enable them—or cause them—to *do* something. Listeners expect an executive speech to be charged with information that has the

power to change the business and the

"Let deeds match words."

PLATUS

lives of those who depend on it for their livelihood, services, or products. A message from a corporate leader has

the potential to *move a market, encourage employees to step up to a new challenge, or calm the fears of an anxious consumer group.* People listen to a corporate leader *expecting* to hear words that in some way give direction to their future.

I realize that most of the work done by top leaders is accomplished in private as they plan and develop strategies. I don't want to give the impression that the primary role of leaders and executives is to make speeches. What I am saying is this: When the decision-making is done, the decisions and strategies must then be presented and articulated to all who bear responsibility for implementing, enacting, or responding to the decisions. The leader is the foremost person to articulate plans, procedures, and vision.

Here is a visual representation of some of the things the top executive must communicate to a wide range of people:

Corporate Mission
↓
Corporate Strategy
↓
Corporate Objectives
↓
Corporate Tactical Plan
↓
Status of Previous Corporate Plans

## EXECUTIVE PRESENTATION GROUPS

Board chairpersons, CEO's, and other top executive leaders regularly address both "external" and "internal" audiences. Various groups, with different perspectives, exist in each audience category.

### External Groups

*The Financial Community.* Executives of publicly traded corporations routinely speak to members of the financial community. They must recognize that *every* speech they give will have an impact on investment bankers and rating agencies, even if their speeches are not made directly to members of these groups. Investors evaluate the words of top executives, along with corporate quarterly reports, global and national economic trends, political trends, and overall market trends, in forming their opinions about public

> Corporate leaders must assume that every word they utter publicly will eventually be heard or read by elements of the financial community.

companies. The words and presentations of a CEO can generate confidence or doubt in the investment community. This audience wants consistency and predictability. It punishes overpromises and surprises.

Executives must recognize that nothing is done or said in a vacuum. Off-the-cuff remarks and extemporaneous presentations by senior executives can have perilous consequences. As a general rule, executives must assume that anything they say will eventually wind up as grist in the mill of the investment community or used by the competition or other special interest groups to influence the image of their organizations. Any words from an executive—both spoken and written—can impact a company's bottom line. Given that an executive's compensation and tenure are heavily influenced by a corporation's stock price, this should be a matter of intense personal concern to *every* executive.

*The Media.* The media can be a minefield of potential disasters or a vehicle to promote the health and success of a business. Information reported by the media is a direct pipeline to the investment community and the public (the consumer). Corporate leaders must remember that media outlets are also profit-hungry businesses. While most media people are concerned with reporting the truth, it is a fact that information sells better when it has a dramatic or even scandalous nature. Bad news always sells better than good news. The media looks first and foremost to a company's leader for *news*.

> "Never interrupt your enemy when he is making a mistake."
>
> NAPOLEON BONAPARTE

*Federal and State Governments and Industry "Watchdogs."* Various government agencies regulate all public corporations in one way or another. Environmental restrictions, safety regulations, equal opportunity laws, rights of the disabled, and the tax codes are only a few government hoops through which corporations must jump daily. Presentations made by corporate executives—whether to internal audiences, general public groups, or directly to government agencies—can have long-term implications for entire industries.

*Trade Associations.* Almost every corporation belongs to one or more trade associations. Effective communication with these associations helps ensure accurate and useful lobbying in the state and federal legislative processes. Associations also serve as a venue for member firms to share valuable information. Executives who address trade groups have an excellent opportunity to launch important industry initiatives or express opinions on issues that transcend the interests of any one company. The executive must always remember, however, that trade groups are closely monitored by government and media groups as sources of information. Remember the general rule mentioned earlier: *Executives must assume that anything they say will eventually wind up as grist for the mill of the investment community.*

## Internal Groups

*Shareholders.* Since the shareholders of a public corporation have ultimate control of the company, executive presentations to this group are sensitive and critical. The annual meeting is typically the only opportunity most shareholders have to see and hear the top leaders of the corporation. For this reason, the executive speech should be created with great care and presented in a dynamic fashion. A corporation's shareholders leave the annual meeting with subjective impressions of the business and the managers of the business. A less than stellar presentation can have a negative impact on stock price and more, regardless of the facts, figures, and information presented.

> "I have often regretted my speech, never my silence."
>
> **XENOCRATES**

*Board of Directors.* Any officer of any major corporation can attest to the importance of having a healthy relationship with the Board of Directors. In their function of executive oversight, Board members can be the greatest imaginable roadblocks to progress, or they can provide the smoothest red carpet ever rolled out before a VIP. The top executive and the senior executive team can add pad to the carpet by doing everything possible to clearly communicate new ideas, project status, and other "state of the company" information.

A top executive's high-quality, well-thought-out presentation can help build the Board's confidence in the entire executive team. This confidence not only will find its way into annual reports and be communicated to shareholders, but also often results in improved stock price and greater decision-making autonomy for the executive team.

*Employees (Current and Retired).* The employees of a corporation want to hear from their leaders, because the top executives of a corporation provide both direction and motivation. Every employee wants to know the long-term goals, objectives, and major initiatives of the organization. They want to hear about new, innovative plans for future products. They want to know what they can expect individually. They want reassurance that the company will be able to provide job security and financial stability. When senior leaders make speeches and presentations to employee groups, these issues and questions are omnipresent in the minds of the listeners. Employees want their leaders to be intelligent, positive, dynamic, and strong. A poor speech or presentation can greatly diminish the confidence employees have in their company's leadership. No executive should ever take an employee group for granted when preparing a speech or presentation.

> No executive should ever take an employee group for granted when preparing a speech or presentation. Familiarity with the group is no excuse for a less-than top-quality presentation.

Current employees are not the only interested "workers." Retired employees who look to company performance for pension or retirement funding are especially concerned with what a top executive has to say. In addressing all employee groups, an executive must keep in mind that familiarity with a group is no excuse for a less-than-top-quality presentation.

*Executive Staff.* Every CEO and senior executive has a staff upon which he depends to execute programs and projects. The senior staff is the closest group of people to the executive and the one with whom the executive interacts most often, both personally and professionally. The familiarity that results from working closely together can sometimes lull a leader into a false sense of security when it comes to being "understood." Communicating with senior staff may be the most important thing a CEO does from an operational perspective. High-quality presentations are a *must.*

One of the now classic success stories of the last century is the rebirth and regeneration of the Chrysler Corporation, brought about by Lee Iacocca. When Iacocca took over the helm at Chrysler, the corporation was in a horrible state. Its products were not competitive, and there seemed to be no hope of improvement. Financially strapped and wounded in almost every strategic area, Chrysler appeared to have a bleak and dismal future. Then along came Mr. Iacocca with a powerful message and the ability to present it effectively. Chrysler became one of the most profitable automobile companies in the world. The "turn-around" of Chrysler in the 1980's and 1990's was largely due to the leadership of Lee Iacocca and his ability to present powerful concepts and ideas in a convincing, easy-to-understand, positive way.

Leaders want enthusiastic support for their ideas and decisions. They want people to embrace their directives and make personal commitments to help turn the corporate vision and goals into reality. The executive speech is the foremost vehicle for garnering a high level of support from all audiences—both internal and external.

# VERY IMPORTANT POINTS

1. All words spoken by all people are *not* equal. The words of top leaders have a powerful impact on people and organizations.

2. When the leader of a business speaks, there is always a response of some kind from many sectors.

3. There are five key elements of business that leaders communicate to a wide range of people:
   - Corporate Mission
   - Corporate Strategy
   - Corporate Objectives
   - Corporate Tactical Plan
   - Status of Previous Corporate Plans

4. Corporate leaders must assume that every word they utter publicly will eventually be heard or read by elements of the financial community.

5. No executive should ever take an employee group for granted when preparing a speech or presentation. Familiarity with the group is no excuse for a less-than-top-quality presentation.

6. The executive speech is the foremost vehicle for garnering a high level of support from all audiences — both internal and external.

# CHAPTER TWO

# THE TEAM CONCEPT

**M**OST BUSY EXECUTIVES ARE TIME-STARVED. A lack of time is perhaps the most significant reason for you to use a team approach for the preparation, design, and delivery of your speeches and presentations. The team concept presented in *Speaking From the Top is* a system of delegation designed to ensure that your message remains uniquely yours and yet is strongly presented. Our goal is to help you hit the mark *every* time!

What is your current method of preparing your speeches and presentations? Do you write and create them yourself? Do you use a speechwriter? How do you ensure that the message you want to deliver will hit the mark, meet the

> "I think there is a world market for maybe five computers."
>
> **THOMAS WATSON, IBM CHAIRMAN, 1943**

objectives, and produce the results you want? How do you know you have the best information to include in your speech? How do you know your presentation devices and tools will be effective for your audience and have the impact you desire? How do you know you are taking advantage of every informational resource available to you? Are your speechwriter and public relations people tapping into the right sources?

Information related to these questions is the heart of this chapter. You may have had at least a few people help you prepare your presentations in the past, but it's also possible that you have done much of this work yourself. In my experiences, I have found that most executives do not use a team approach to the extent they could or should. The stakes in the global marketplace require the effective, powerful, and easily understandable presentation of ideas and complicated concepts *every time* an executive speaks to a group. A delegated and focused team approach is today's best method for speech preparation.

> A delegated and focused team approach is today's best method for speech preparation.

## EXCEEDING AUDIENCE EXPECTATIONS

The most important events for a corporation as a whole are often the speeches and presentations of the company's top leaders. Audience expectations for these presentations tend to run very high. Usually, there is some advance notice about the subject matter of the speech, either through official channels or through the company grapevine. Attendees talk among themselves about what they expect to see and hear. Will they hear about the issues and concerns they have? Will they receive valuable information to help them be more effective in their jobs? Will they walk away from the talk (whether given in person or via closed circuit television, satellite uplink, or webcast) with the image of a strong, dynamic, and credible leader freshly imprinted in their minds? Or will they leave disappointed? Will they hear what they hoped to hear? Will the presentation be dull, lifeless, and boring—or exciting and energizing?

**"THE TRUTH SQUAD."** An interesting group emerged during the presidential debates between Vice-President Al Gore and Governor George W. Bush. This group debuted on one of the major networks as "the Truth Squad." These individuals were armed with high-speed Internet access, transcripts from past speeches, and calculators to scrutinize every point of fact uttered by each candidate. At the end of the debate, the candidates received a rating on a truth scale.

> "640K ought to be enough for anybody."
>
> **BILL GATES**

As time goes on, I believe that similar, formalized truth squads will become more and more commonplace. Meanwhile, it is significant for the top executive to realize that a "truth squad" exists right now in every audience he or she addresses. Audiences of all types are listening, with what Gerry Spence calls "invisible credibility feelers," for candor, credibility, and accuracy of "factual" information. In this light, even inadvertently mis-spoken statistics can backfire. Recognize that your audience expects rock-solid reliability and absolute accuracy from you.

## FACE UP TO YOUR OWN COMPETENCY

While coaching top-level executives from some of America's largest corporations over the years, I discovered they all came into the coaching process with one thing in common: They suffered from "unconscious incompetence" regarding their presentations. In other words, they "didn't know what they didn't know" when it came to creating and delivering a great speech. Top executives are some of the most intelligent people I've ever known, and to say they are brilliant is not an exaggeration. Intelligence, however, is not enough. Having a good track record is not enough. Being well liked is not enough. Being well connected and respected is not enough. None of these leaders were making full use of the tools and resources available that could help them deliver the outstanding speeches and presentations that audiences expect.

While coaching top-level executives from some of America's largest corporations over the years, I discovered they all came into the coaching process with one thing in common: They "didn't know what they didn't know" when it came to creating and delivering a great speech. None of these leaders were making full use of the tools and resources available that could help them deliver the outstanding speeches and presentations that audiences expect.

My coaching process is extensive. I immerse myself in the needs of my customers. In doing so, I learn a lot about the people I'm coaching, the industries in which they work, and the audiences they address. I am able to give honest feedback about their prior speeches and presentations and evaluate the image that has been established. There is nothing worse for the image of an executive than the delivery of a dull, lifeless, poorly planned, or poorly delivered speech. I'm sure you agree, especially as you think back over the years when you were listening to messages from your superiors.

Sadly, top executives often do not anticipate the high expectations of their audiences. Even more sadly, they do not recognize they are boring or speaking in a monotone. They do not receive honest, critical feedback from their people; therefore, they do not know their true need for improvement. After interviewing hundreds of people from organizations across our nation, I have found that the majority of individuals who sit through executive speeches are hard pressed to remember the content of the messages they have heard. They can recall, however, bad deliveries and lifeless presentations from particular executives. Furthermore, they interpret poor presentations as a failure or shortcoming in leadership.

Your audiences expect you to be a good speaker. Don't disappoint them!

## QUALITY PRESENTATIONS SELL

One thing you should remember is that you are always selling something when you make a speech or presentation. The sale may involve a plan, a strategy, an idea, or a theory, but you really do want your audience to "buy in" to your message. And yes, you are also selling yourself and your leadership ability.

Would you send your sales team out to make a multi-million-dollar proposal to a customer without the best presentation tools and information available? Or would you rather it create a high quality presentation that would dazzle the prospect and demolish the competition? High quality presentations sell!

> Audiences interpret poor presentations as a failure or shortcoming in leadership.

Why not expect the same for your own speeches and presentations? Think about this: How many dollars are spent in training budgets to help your sales team be successful? Think of all the effort and energy that go into launching new products and services. What about the budgets for advertising to position a product with potential customers? Now consider how little you may be investing to make your own speeches and presentations as powerful as possible.

Top quality presentations do more than sell. They also instill confidence. Employees, top-level lieutenants, Wall Street analysts, shareholders, and the general public want their preferred corporate leaders to be strong, bold, and decisive. Employees and shareholders alike want to believe their leaders know what they are doing. When confidence runs high, the "troops" rally behind their leaders and enthusiastically follow them. As an executive, you need to recognize that every speech you make is an opportunity to build confidence. Every speech you make impacts your image as a leader who is dynamic, trustworthy, and on the cutting edge.

> Your audiences expect you to be a good speaker. Don't disappoint them!

## USE YOUR RESOURCES

How is all of this accomplished? How do you project the image, hit the mark, exceed expectations, instill trust and confidence, and *inspire* your audience every time out? As great as you are, you can't do it alone—it takes a team effort.

Simply stated, the team concept of preparation is a system that ensures that you have tapped every resource available to you in the preparation of your speeches. Every large corporation has many divisions or departments, each with its many talented people who possess a great deal of valuable information and technical expertise. My experience has led me to conclude that most leaders rarely use all the talent and resources available to them within their own organizations.

The executive needs to consider three important factors in choosing his or her team to help create a speech. I refer to these factors as the CPA model:

- C = Content
- P = Presentation Setting
- A = Audience

CONTENT. A successful presentation centers on focused content objectives. Start with a tightly crafted, *written* list of your top three objectives. Know what you want to accomplish and how what you are going to say relates to the audience.

> Consider how little you may be investing to make your own speeches and presentations as powerful as possible.

PRESENTATION SETTING. Next, nail down the presentation constraints. Will the speech be live or taped? Will it be in a large facility or a small boardroom? Will the speech be delivered in friendly territory or on hostile turf? Will there be a question-and-answer session? Will teleprompters be used? Gather all the information you can about the setting for your speech and the technical support that may be available.

AUDIENCE. Define your specific audience. Who will be there? Also define any secondary audiences. Who will hear second-hand what you have said?

After you have thoroughly identified these CPA factors, begin to choose your presentation team. Choose people who can help you address your specific objectives. Choose the technical support to help you make the most of the presentation setting. Choose those with astute insight into the nature of the audience.

Let me give you a brief overview of a typical presentation development team.

## THE TEAM

Generally speaking, the team should be small, yet have access to the entire organization. In many ways, the ideal team is like a production crew for the making of a movie. Let's look at some suggested positions for the team:

1. TEAM COORDINATOR **(THE PRODUCER).** Someone must manage the efforts of the team. Depending on the amount of time you have available, you may want to do this job yourself. If not, you should appoint someone who has good management skills and a solid working knowledge of the entire organization. Most importantly, the person should know YOU. This should also be a person with whom you can communicate easily and who understands thoroughly your goals and objectives for the company. This person should feel free to give you honest feedback—good and bad. This person might be a longstanding veteran of the corporation whom you trust and respect. Or you might want to select an agency or a communications company. I have filled this role for many executives myself. Choose a can-do person who will get the job done.

"Experience is simply the name we give our mistakes."

OSCAR WILDE

2. GRAPHICS AND MULTIMEDIA COORDINATOR **(SPECIAL EFFECTS DIRECTOR).** This slot should be filled by someone who has an excellent understanding of cutting-edge presentation technology, the technical capabilities of your company, and the technical constraints of the meeting or event. If something of a technical nature is needed, this is the person who would know what, where, and how to get it. He or she should be creative but also know how to mesh creativity with clarity in communication, and should understand how to *sell* a presentation. Don't be reluctant to outsource this to a

supplier if your company doesn't have marketing communications expertise in-house.

3. CONTENT SPECIALIST **(RESEARCH ASSISTANT).** This person should be an information repository who is very familiar with every aspect of your business and your industry. If you need statistical information for your speech, this person should know where to find it. If you need sales, marketing or product information, this person will know where it can be found. If you need financial data, this person should be able to get it. If you need market data or demographic

> "Don't bog down your speech with a lot of numbers and statistics that people won't remember or will misinterpret."
>
> TOM SLONE

information, this is the person to track it down. This position requires a creative person with a broad knowledge of your industry and your corporate practices.

---

I suggest the use of "back-up books" and "back-up book operators" whenever appropriate. Back-up books are big binders—tabbed for easy reference—or a specially loaded laptop computer that contains all the information that might be needed to answer questions. A back-up book operator is a nimble and knowledgeable assistant who sits near the executive and finds needed information quickly during Q&A segments. The Content Specialist is the ideal person to man this station. As with most things in life, however, there are pros and cons to back-up books. Pro: the book gives you a measure of confidence that your facts are straight. Con: if you have the book, there is no place to hide. You can't say, "I don't have that data with me."

---

4. SPEECHWRITER/PRESENTATION CREATOR **(SCREENPLAY WRITER).** This is someone who works closely with you to create your speech or presentation script. The writer must gather information and data collected by other team members

and put it into a meaningful and easily understood format, using your language and personality "style." If you have the time and skill, you may want to do the writing yourself. If not, select a professional to help you. It is said in a legal context that "the man who represents himself has a fool for a lawyer." The same principle is usually true when it comes to speechwriting. Most executives can't take the time to craft a truly great speech. They can dictate the major points they want to address and turn the actual writing over to a professional writer. If the speechwriter is short on humor, you may also want to consult with a humorist. A clever line can add spice and keep an audience's attention level high.

> "Tact is the ability to describe others as they see themselves."
>
> ABRAHAM LINCOLN

5. PRESENTATION COACH (THE DIRECTOR). An outside coach is essential if you want to maximize your success as a presenter. An outside presentation coach can look at you and your team with objective eyes. A coach is especially helpful when it comes to the actual delivery of your presentation. Practice in advance of the speech is critical, and a good coach can be invaluable to you at the practice stage. Even the best athletes use coaches to perform at higher levels. The speech coach is ideally on the sidelines at show time; but his or her work appears on stage, just a tennis coach's work shows up on the center court at Wimbledon.

Depending on the event, your presentation team can be large or small. You might incorporate two functions into one position, or you may want to wear one or more of the hats yourself. Also, teams can be "virtual"—not everyone must be physically present, and they don't have to be involved on a full-time basis. The key is to bring in the right people at the right time for the right assignments for the right duration. The important thing is be sure the functional categories are covered and that each role is filled by a person who has the necessary expertise, background, and desire to help you.

## TEAM CONTRIBUTIONS

What should you expect from your team? Your team should supply you with:

1. INFORMATION AND STATISTICS. Every speech or presentation transmits information of some kind—technical, financial, procedural, conceptual, or general. The information in your speech must be accurate, to the point, and the most current available. It should support the goals and objectives of your speech.

Your team should collect all the information you need for your speech or presentation. You as the executive should be the one to understand and control the degree of "spin" put on the facts at hand. Your credibility can be permanently wiped out by clumsy manipulation or selective use of data. At the other end of the spectrum, too much data with no spin can be perceived by audiences as confusing, ponderous and boring—the balance has to be struck

2. GRAPHICS AND MULTIMEDIA SUPPORT. What was considered high-tech audiovisual just a few years ago is considered low-tech today. Challenge your team to use cutting-edge presentation technology.

> "Man will occasionally stumble over the truth, but most times he will pick himself up and carry on."
>
> **WINSTON CHURCHILL**

3. **TECHNICAL AND LOGISTICAL SUPPORT.** Direct your team to make certain that every piece of technical equipment needed for your presentation is in place and checked out thoroughly, and that back-up systems are in place (from bulbs to fuses to mechanics to cords). Expect your team to give you detailed information about the facility and the presentation environment.

4. **COACHING.** The coach you select should challenge you—yes, even *demand* that you deliver a powerful presentation. A good coach is an expert on order, flow, and pacing. A good coach should understand the mind of the audience. A professional coach will train you to showcase YOU and help you deliver the most dynamic presentation possible. I really want to emphasize that the coach should come into the development process fairly early—ideally to support the writer in tailoring the content to the speaker's natural talents, and no later than the first read-through of the speech. Dress rehearsal time is often too late. There's much less a coach can do at that stage to correct flaws or pump up a delivery style.

## USING YOUR TEAM

Subsequent chapters of *Speaking From the Top* will provide more detail about actually using your team, but I want to give you a brief overview here. The team needs to be sized and staffed to fit the work at hand, and not overdone so as to complicate matters. I recommend a simple project management approach. Begin with a list of key elements and the people and activities that must be managed from conception of a presentation to technical teardown after an event. Here is a starting list:

| # | Activity/Position | Contribution |
|---|---|---|
| 1 | Administrative Assistants | Keeping track of operational details, schedules, appointments |
| 2 | Advertising Agencies | Promotional pieces, publicity, TV commercials, out-takes |
| 3 | Attorneys | Contracts and agreements |
| 4 | Camera Operators | Taping and video production |
| 5 | Coach | Linking everything, bringing out your best |
| 6 | Communications People | Telephone services, web connections |
| 7 | Graphics Technicians | Slides, charts, graphs |
| 8 | Meeting Coordinators | Schedules, facilities, and itineraries |
| 9 | Music Directors | Music |
| 10 | Other Senior Executives | Support or co-speakers |
| 11 | Producers | Program production |
| 12 | Public Relations | Press releases |
| 13 | Speechwriters | Speech preparation |
| 14 | Stage Crews | Props and equipment handling, sound and lighting |
| 15 | Technical Support | Equipment operation (teleprompter) |
| 16 | Translators | Foreign language interpretation/translation |

The list could go on. Your key task as leader is to choose the coordinator or manager who can work with all groups and make certain that all tasks are accomplished timely, efficiently and with excellence. Each member of your team should be held accountable for his or her logical portion of the process.

By creating a specialized team, you will be able to tap effectively into the expertise of your organization, which is no doubt considerable. Set yourself to become fully aware of all the information and support that is available to you. If you have a video department, you might want to consider its ability to put clips together that can demonstrate years of history in three very interesting minutes. With its visual impact, such a video may save you 10–12 minutes of speaking. Your Public Relations Department no doubt has access to news clips, articles, and other information that can add both substance and interest to your speeches. Your corporation's advertising agency may have TV commercials, out-takes, and other footage that can add "entertainment" value and humor to your remarks. Your goal is to identify a team that can acquire the content and provide the communication expertise to produce a complete presentation package for you.

> "If you have an important point to make, don't try to be subtle or clever. Use a pile driver. Hit the point once. Then come back and hit it again. Then hit it a third time—a tremendous whack."
>
> **WINSTON CHURCHILL**

## CREATE A TOTAL PACKAGE

When you deliver a speech, you are delivering far more than a collection of words and sentences. You are delivering a total message that includes words, visual effects, audio effects, and an intangible aura that will either build up or detract from your image as a leader. Your audiences have a high expectation level for your messages, and you can't afford to disappoint them. I believe your goal should be to EXCEED their expectations every time! A good team, with a good coach at the helm, gives you an added ability to do that much more easily.

# VERY IMPORTANT POINTS

1. Use a team approach to elevate the quality of your presentations.

2. When you deliver a speech, you are delivering a total message that includes words, visual effects, audio effects, and an intangible aura that will either build up or detract from your image as a leader.

3. Quality presentations "sell."
   - Begin with clear, written objectives
   - Every speech is an opportunity to build confidence and impact your image as a leader who is dynamic, trustworthy, and on the cutting edge
   - When confidence runs high, the "troops" rally behind their leaders and enthusiastically follow them

4. Remember three important factors, using the CPA model:
   - C—Develop relevant *content*. Have written objectives.
   - P—Analyze the *presentation* venue.
   - A—Define your *audience*.

5. Keep your team small and focused. The key is to bring in the right people at the right time for the right assignments for the right duration. Be sure the functional categories are covered and that each role is filled by a person who has the necessary expertise, background, and desire to help you.

6. Use all of your available resources to create the best Executive Presentation Team
   - Team Coordinator
   - Graphics and Multimedia Coordinator
   - Content Specialist
   - Speechwriter
   - Personal Presentation Coach

7. Team contributions include:
   - Information and statistics
   - Graphics and multimedia
   - Technical support
   - Coaching for superior delivery—often the real key to success

# CHAPTER THREE

# CONFIDENCE

J UST BECAUSE A PERSON IS A SENIOR executive and a leader of hundreds or even thousands of people is no guarantee that anxiety won't rear its ugly head when a speech or public presentation is imminent. Public speaking remains one of the top fears for human beings, and there is no immunity granted to anyone, regardless of title, position, or authority. The antidote for this kind of anxiety is *preparation-based confidence.*

You may think a discussion of confidence in a book addressed to some of the most confident people in the world would be unnecessary. I thought the same way until I started coaching "confident" people. Because senior executives often have worked their way to the top over a long period of time, they tend to have more experience with public speaking than most people. But they still experience anxiety and confidence issues about their presentations. In many instances, the confidence and anxiety issues for senior executives may even be more serious because audience expectations about what they say and how they say it are higher. Top executives also tend to be more sensitive to the need for balancing their messages to reach a wide variety of constituencies who may have widely diverging viewpoints. Striking the right balance without turning the message to mush is reasonable cause for some nervousness.

> "Whatever course you decide upon, there is always someone to tell you that you are wrong. There are always difficulties arising which tempt you to believe that your critics are right. To map out a course of action and follow it to an end requires courage."
>
> **RALPH WALDO EMERSON**

Let's face it. Every time a top executive makes a speech, he or she is exposed to critical analysis, judgement and second-guessing. Certainly the executive's personal image is on the line. In some instances, a poor speech or presentation can be the beginning of serious problems for the business itself. This reality is enough to create a lot of knee-knocking anxiety for any normally courageous leader. High-stakes speeches and presentations can produce high anxiety in anyone, regardless of experience or stature.

Recently, I was sitting next to a partner in a large investment firm. I was telling him about this book and how I thought it would help senior executives create and deliver better presentations. He was very excited to hear about the things I planned to write, and he confirmed how important executive presentations are to his profession. He said about his own firm, "I will stay with them even when times are tough if the message from the CEO is confident and strong. I like executives who can inspire confidence." For me, this says it all.

The Merriam-Webster definition of the word "confidence" clearly indicates that confidence is rooted in our feelings and in our emotions: It is "a feeling or consciousness of one's powers or of reliance on one's circumstances."

To understand why an impending speech or presentation has the power to play havoc with your feelings, you have to have a basic understanding of fear. Fear can be the most destructive of all our emotions, and it has the power to severely impact performance in every aspect of your life. Fear is also the main emotion at work when it comes to speechmaking. I certainly don't claim to be an expert on fear, but I know what creates fear and I know why it's a problem when you have to make a speech.

Fear may be the most powerful emotion people experience, with the exception of love. The amazing thing about fear is that it usually results from something we are thinking may happen in the future. In other words, we can become fearful and anxious when we start thinking about things that have not yet happened. The future is fertile ground for both worry and fear. When

> Turn all the "unknowns" into "knowns" to erase fear and raise confidence.

our minds engage the many possibilities associated with future events, we seem to gravitate to the negative possibilities more than the positive. It is when we *focus* on negative future possibilities that fear begins to take root.

Obviously, a certain amount of fear is healthy. Fear is a God-given emotion and is designed to protect us from potential harm. A healthy fear can help you anticipate future problems and difficulties, and in turn, help you plan better and achieve greater results. When it comes to making an important speech, anticipating the concerns of the audience—perhaps even the hostility of the audience—and the constraints of the venue can

generate a healthy fear that leads to taking preemptive meas-
ures to avoid giving a poor presentation. A friend of mine who
recently retired as the top executive for a large public corporation here in Dallas sums up this point well: "One needs to be
*intense* without being *tense* when preparing and presenting a
speech."

However, if fear and anxiety are not resolved and satisfied
before the speech is delivered, the overall confidence level of the
speaker is likely to be less than desirable. At the time the speech
is made, a lack of confidence can show itself in nervousness,
poor voice inflection, negative body language, and other visual
and auditory distractions. In severe cases of low confidence, the
visual evidence of fear may be so strong that the audience
becomes more interested in the emotional state of the presenter
than the content of the message. I trust you have never experienced anything so extreme, but my guess is that you are no
stranger to some pre-speech jitters and maybe even a good
dose of fear. Conversely, when fear and anxiety levels drop, the
result is higher confidence and a greater projection of strength.

I believe there is nothing more effective than a confident
speaker or presenter. A confident speaker exudes an intangible
aura of self-assurance that impacts listeners in a powerful way.
When a speaker is confident, his or her words *sound* more
truthful and the speaker appears more
trustworthy. Certainly I am not saying
that leaders routinely lie or attempt to
con their audiences. Rather, I'm saying that speakers who are less than
confident generate questions about
the truthfulness and credibility of their messages. As a top
executive, you know how crucial credibility is. To appear less
than credible is a nightmare scenario.

> A confident speaker exudes
> an intangible aura of self-
> assurance that impacts
> listeners in a powerful way.

## A PREPARATION TEAM BUILDS CONFIDENCE

As we discussed in previous chapters, the demands for a good executive speech are many. There are dozens of details that can impact the executive's presentation, and many of them can give rise to fear. To illustrate this point, let's look at a scenario that every businessperson has experienced: a sales presentation made before a group of people who are making a buying decision. As an executive, you

> Every speech you make is a sales presentation of sorts.

have no doubt participated in many such presentations. Furthermore, every speech you make is a sales presentation of sorts.

Let's imagine we are gathered in a room with others who will hear a series of presentations on a certain type of product we are thinking of buying. Let's assume the product in question is expensive and complicated. Three presenters have been allotted thirty minutes each to demonstrate their products and convince you of their products' superiority.

**SALES PRESENTATION #1.** The sales person arrives about ten minutes prior to the presentation with a cart full of technical equipment. The next twenty minutes are spent looking for electrical plugs, extension cords, and a way to make his laptop computer project the proper image on a display device. The presentation begins, and the sales person clicks through a canned slide show, never pausing or deviating from his prepared script. The sales person appears to be confident about the product being presented but is not too sure of his presentation equipment. In fact, his operation of the equipment is awkward and his body language indicates that he would rather be doing something else.

**SALES PRESENTATION #2.** The presenter arrives at the appointed time, opens a briefcase, and removes a stack of transparencies.

The presenter asks if you have an overhead projector. An overhead projector is provided, and the presentation moves forward smoothly. The sales person deftly changes transparencies in the proper sequence. The presentation eventually concludes, and the sales person turns off the overhead projector. You are invited to ask questions. After a short period of polite conversation, the sales person asks for your business, packs up the transparencies, and leaves the room.

SALES PRESENTATION #3. The sales person arrives, accompanied by a couple of other people. While the sales person casually strolls about the room introducing himself to you and your group, the two helpers are quickly assembling a combination of items at the front of the room. In less than three minutes, the equipment is ready and the presentation begins. The helpers distribute professionally prepared handouts to your group. The sales professional executes a seamless presentation, using multi-media, color slides, transparencies, and a flip chart. The presentation seems effortless, and the message is well coordinated and powerfully clear. Credibility and professionalism permeate the room, and your buying decision is about to be made.

> If you don't know where you're going, you'll end up someplace else.
>
> YOGI BERRA

Obviously Sales Presentation #3 is the superior presentation and the one that has the greatest impact. Your company buys from Company #3. What is the essential difference here? Confidence! The sales person arrived with help to handle the technical production. Time was available to meet you and your group and shake hands. The smooth flow of the information and the ease of presentation convinced you these people were competent. You concluded, "These are the kind of people with whom we want to work." Their product seemed to have the greatest credibility. The confidence of the sales person translated as honesty and professional integrity.

Why was the sales person in this third scenario more confident? Very likely because he had rehearsed his presentation several times and was comfortable with both the content and the technology he would be using. His words and body movements were coordinated, and there was no action that distracted from the message. He *knew* he was going to present a technologically superior presentation with no mistakes because his technical crew had planned and rehearsed its role as well. When presenters are personally confident and their presentations come off without a hitch, you can bet that they have a good team behind them!

Selling an idea, strategy, service, or product is usually a primary objective in an executive's message. In the sales scenarios provided above, the salesperson had to contend with only a few elements compared to what most executives face, but the principle is the same. The sales person who was part of a team did the best job!

Building on the five core areas of team responsibility, let's take a brief look at how each role can add to your confidence as a speechmaker.

1. TEAM COORDINATOR. The general manager of your team should give you periodic updates about your presentation project. These updates should include matters related to speech content, venue constraints, and audience concerns. Schedule these updates at the time you designate your presentation team. The more you are assured that things are on track, the greater your overall confidence.

2. GRAPHICS AND MULTIMEDIA COORDINATOR. Review with your graphics coordinator all of the materials that are to be visually displayed as you speak. Ask about back-up systems. The

greater the familiarity you have with the *visual* content of your presentation, and the greater your confidence in the expertise of your technical team, the more confidence you will feel.

3. **CONTENT SPECIALIST.** Knowing that you have the best, most complete, and most current information available for your speech is a powerful confidence builder.

4. **SPEECHWRITER/PRESENTATION CREATOR.** When you have a professional writer help you craft your speech, you will have greater confidence that your line of thought is going to come through strong and clear.

5. **PRESENTATIONS COACH.** Your coach will rehearse you with the eye of a professional, evaluating the entire package. The technology, the content, the message, and how you deliver it will be scrutinized by your coach. When your rehearsals are over, you will KNOW you will be a success, and that is the greatest confidence builder of all. There is no fear in certainty.

> Knowing that you will be successful is the greatest confidence builder of all.

# VERY IMPORTANT POINTS

1. Public speaking is one of the top fears of human beings. The antidote for fear is confidence. Confidence comes from turning those "unknowns" into "knowns."

2. Fear reveals itself in presentations as nervousness, poor voice tone/inflection, and negative body language.

3. Displays of fear destroy credibility.

4. The right preparation team can build your confidence in practical and highly significant ways.

5. When fear and anxiety levels drop, the result is higher confidence and greater projection of strength.

6. When presenters are personally confident and their presentations come off without a hitch, you can bet that they have a good team behind them.

7. Knowing that you will be successful is the greatest confidence builder of all.

# CHAPTER FOUR

# ESTABLISHING PRESENTATION OBJECTIVES

THE BEST WAY TO ENSURE THE SUCCESS of a journey is to know in advance where you are going. Every good presentation has specific objectives—an arrival point. Regardless of the group you will address, you should develop specific, clearly stated goals. What are your desired outcomes? What do you hope to accomplish? What do you want your audience members to have when they leave? Just exactly what should your message convey?

I use a funneling process as a tool to determine the objectives of a presentation. I developed this funneling process many years ago, and it was featured in my first book, *Inspire Any Audience* (Honor Books, 1997). It is a time-tested method for assembling and bringing order to the many factors that impact a presentation.

**Information Goes in the Top Here and Is Funneled Down Through the Steps**

**1. Determine the action** you want your audience to take.
  • Ask yourself, "What action do I want my audience to take as a result of my presentation?"
  • Ask yourself, "What must the participants know, say, and do differently when they leave my presentation?"

**2. Define your audience.**
  • You must know the audience very well.
  • Ask yourself, "What are the skills, knowledge, and attitudes of my audience?"
  • What are the positions represented in the audience?

**3. Brainstorm to determine:** • Your needs
  • Your audience's needs  • Any third-party needs

**4. Focus these various desires**—work them into three or four *written* objectives, keeping in mind that participants want practical, usable knowledge.
  • Keep objectives short.
  • Write out in one sentence what you want to accomplish. Refer to it often.

**5. Test your objectives mentally** by putting yourself in the audience's shoes. Once you've defined your audience, check your objectives from their perspective.

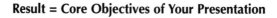

**Result = Core Objectives of Your Presentation**

The funneling process does exactly what it says. It involves the collection of information to drop into the top of an imaginary information funnel. The information then filters down to the small end of the funnel through several simple steps. What emerges at the bottom of the funnel are clear core objectives.

**STEP 1: DETERMINE THE ACTION.** What action do you want your audience to take as a result of your presentation? What do you desire your audience members to know, say, and do differently when they leave your presentation? What are your desired changes in attitude and behavior? What do you envision as the impact on your corporation?

**STEP 2: DEFINE YOUR AUDIENCE.** What are the skills, knowledge, and incoming attitudes of your audience toward you, your company and your subject matter? What positions and spheres of influence are represented in your audience? What specific issues are likely to be on the minds of your audience members? Is the group diverse or homogeneous?

**STEP 3: BRAINSTORM TO DETERMINE NEEDS.** What are your needs? What are your audience's needs? Should any third-party needs be considered?

**STEP 4: FOCUS THE NEEDS INTO OBJECTIVES.** Write down all of your objectives, keeping in mind that audience members want practical, usable knowledge. Keep your objectives short—you should be able to state each objective with one sentence. Use action verbs. Most effective speeches deal with only three to five objectives. If you have more objectives, you may need to plan more than one presentation. Audiences are only able to absorb a limited set of concepts at one sitting.

> A man can only attain knowledge with the help of those who possess it. This must be understood from the very beginning. One must learn from him who knows.
>
> GEORGE GURDJIEFF

**STEP 5: TEST YOUR OBJECTIVES.** Put yourself in your audience members' shoes and check your objectives from their perspectives. Adjust your objectives to meet audience needs and questions.

After you complete these five steps, you should have the core objectives for your speech and be ready to move forward in creating the actual presentation.

## THE MESSAGE

Let's look at the specific kinds of information that go into the funnel to make the process work. The first involves the nature of the message itself. Will your presentation be made to an internal or external group? Obviously, presentations for people on your corporate team will have different parameters and objectives than a speech to be delivered to an external group. Also, you may want to strike a more informal tone with an internal audience.

Next, determine the type of message you want to send. There are essentially four types of messages:

1. MESSAGES OF INFLUENCE. A message of influence must convince people of something in a way that will motivate them and cause a change in their behavior. You may want your managers and people to adopt new methods or procedures. You may want people to buy into your vision or your mission. There are many subjects of influence, but they all involve motivating the audience to some kind of action.

> A day . . . is a miniature eternity.
>
> RALPH WALDO EMERSON

2. MESSAGES OF INFORMATION AND EDUCATION. Informational messages are designed to transfer knowledge and improve the skills of an audience. An informational or educational presentation involves the explanation of concepts and principles. The use of graphics and visual tools can be especially important in these presentations.

3. MESSAGES OF INSPIRATION. An inspirational message can have several different objectives. You may want to motivate your audience to adopt new attitudes. You may be trying to "recharge" your audience or build morale. An inspirational

message tends to involve the emotions, and the use of real-life stories can be very effective.

4. MESSAGES OF AN IMPROMPTU/EMERGENCY NATURE. Usually, you have little or no time to prepare for these "do it now" speeches. Often the media is present and, in many cases, these messages involve a crisis or a serious problem. The Ford and Firestone Tire disaster of 2000 is a good example. And most everyone remembers the problem of "contaminated" Tylenol many years ago. The more cohesive your presentation team is, the greater its ability to prepare instant messages to address emergencies or crises.

Each presentation may contain one or more of the above characteristics. Identify each type of message that applies to your event.

## UNDERSTANDING YOUR AUDIENCE

As I have stated previously, understanding your audience is critical to the success of your presentation. Too many speakers assume all audiences are the same and that the same presentation should work for each one. Others make the mistake of assuming that a particular audience has the same profile from year to year or from event to event. These miscalculations are the main reasons speakers "bomb." I strongly believe that every audience is unique. It is your responsibility to understand your audience and adapt your presentation accordingly.

For example, let's assume you are scheduled to present new information to two groups—a group of sales people and a group of engineers. These two groups are going to have different "personalities." The individuals within the two groups are likely to process information in different ways. Sales people are going to respond more favorably to a presentation that has good entertainment value and hearty doses of humor and real-life stories. Engineers are likely to want just the facts without a lot of extraneous anecdotal information. Lists, tables, and charts are usually very effective presentation tools for engineers.

Never assume that the same speech should be delivered to each audience with equal results. A good speech is a good speech. But your speech can be more *effective* and *significantly improved* if you tailor it to your specific audience. If two highly diverse audience segments are likely to be included in the same event, you may be wise to schedule *two* speeches— tailoring your message to target specific concerns and objectives for each segment.

Challenge your team to help you determine the characteristics of your audience. Create a checklist or profile of the typical attendee. Here are just a few items you might identify:

- Gender
- Age
- Types of work the person does
- Average income level
- Level of education
- Paramount interests and concerns
- Likes and dislikes (to the best of your knowledge)
- How does he or she feel about the topic you are going to discuss?

The information you can gather about your audience is endless, but these are the most significant traits to consider. Analyze this information closely before you enter the speechwriting process—even before you complete your objectives.

Third, ask yourself, "Why does this particular audience need to hear *me*?" Many speakers never question whether their audiences need to hear what they have to say. While it may be true at times that your audience members are required to sit through your speech, it will be much more effective if you determine WHY they need to hear what YOU will be saying! My opinion is that if you can't figure out why your audience needs to hear you, you are going to waste a great many man-hours, including your own.

Only after you have determined who your audience is and why they need to hear what you have to say can you be in a position to decide what kind of presentation will have the greatest impact. Core information can be transmitted in a wide variety of ways. Presentation technology today allows a speaker to insert and interchange blocks of data and graphics quickly and easily. Every audience is different. Every presentation should be, too.

Finally, recognize that every person in your audience has seven basic subconscious desires. These are:

1. The desire to belong
2. The desire to be respected
3. The desire to be liked
4. The desire to be safe
5. The desire to succeed
6. The desire to find romance
7. The desire to be inspired

Understanding these seven desires can help you mold your presentation to touch your audience members as *human beings*—not merely business associates.

## WHAT RESPONSE DO YOU EXPECT?

You can expect three levels of response from your audience. Each level builds on the preceding one. Your challenge as a speaker is to move your audience through each level progressively. The ultimate result you desire may only require movement through one or two levels, or it may require you to take the audience through every level. This is a determination you must make, and your presentation should be designed to take the audience through each stage in sequence.

STAGE 1—BUY IN. This is the first stage of response in every presentation. You must hook your audience members and move them into a mind-set of accepting—at least in a general way—the ideas you are presenting. This requires giving them information they know is true from their own experience. At this stage, presenting information that addresses one or more of their seven subconscious desires will help you achieve buy-in.

> If you can't feed a hundred people, then feed just one.
>
> **MOTHER TERESA**

Buy-in is complete when your audience acknowledges that your remarks have value and that you are worthy of their continued attention. This is the minimal response a speaker should seek to evoke.

STAGE 2—APPROVAL. At this stage you want your audience not only to acknowledge that your presentation has value and meaning, but also to enthusiastically embrace your message. This is the stage where you create "believers." There are three aspects of this process. First, audience members must accept your version of the "facts." Then they must accept your "logic flow," or the conceptual path you are using to present your ideas. Finally, they must agree with your message at the gut level. It's often easy to get agreement on facts and logic flow and then lose the audience. Generally, this happens if the audience has strongly held values or prejudices unrelated to "facts."

Approval occurs when you see nodding heads and confident, responsive faces beaming back at you. If you see people staring blankly at you with arms crossed, you are not creating approval and you may have never achieved buy-in.

STAGE 3—ACTION. It is very difficult to motivate an audience to action. Know that going in. If you want your audience members to take voluntary action, you will have to sell them on doing so. The "action" you define can vary from spending money to investing "emotional capital" in a specific decision.

> Flattery is all right so long as you don't inhale.
>
> **ADLAI STEVENSON**

Every speech or presentation does not require action. If this is the level of response you desire, however, recognize that you need to spell out specifically what you desire each audience member to do—state clearly the when, how, where and why. Make sure a procedure is in place to facilitate the action you challenge them to take. Recognize that most "actions" should be taken in the immediate future, as in *now*.

## FOCUS

Direct your team to take the information gathered thus far and distill it into a list of stated needs. I recommend that you take a piece of paper and make two columns. Put "Audience" at the top of one column and "Me" at the top of the other column. Then list the essential needs for both you and your audience. When you have completed the two lists, compare them and focus on the common ground. Also note the most *important* needs.

Think about possible ways you might satisfy both the common needs and the important needs. Then answer these four questions. Keep your answers simple and to the point, and put them in writing.

- Why am I giving this speech or presentation?
- What's in it for my audience?
- What is the purpose of the presentation (to influence, inform, inspire, or all of these)?
- What specific action do I want my audience to take after the presentation?
- How will I know my speech was successful?

Once you have answered these questions (using all of the information you have collected and placed in the funnel), develop your objectives. In writing objectives, use short, concise phrases that begin with an action word (i.e., determine, communicate, share). Analyze your presentation objectives further by asking these three questions:

1. What will be the actual content of the presentation?
2. How detailed must the information be, and how long should the presentation last?
3. How will audience members benefit by taking the action I desire them to take?

Adjust your objectives to reflect your answers. The final step in clarifying your objectives is to ask these questions:

1. Are my objectives clear?
2. Do I know what I want to accomplish and how I want to accomplish it?

3. Do I know why I want to accomplish it?

4. Do my objectives give the audience good reasons to listen?

Clear objectives are the foundation of a great presentation. Without objectives, a presentation will lack focus, direction and value. Your objectives should be short and well focused and should answer the basic question in the back of *every* audience member's mind: "What's in it for me?"

> Results! Why, man,
> I have gotten a lot of results.
> I know several thousand
> things that won't work.
>
> **THOMAS EDISON**

# VERY IMPORTANT POINTS

1. Every presentation should be built upon a foundation of specific objectives.

2. Use the funneling process to build your objectives:
   - Determine the action you want the audience to take
   - Define your audience
   - Brainstorm to determine all needs
   - Focus needs into objectives
   - Test your objectives (by yourself, mentally, then with others close to you)

3. Determine the type of presentation you are making:
   - Internal or external
   - Message of influence
   - Message of information and education
   - Message of inspiration
   - Emergency or impromptu message

4. Know your audience:
   - Gender
   - Age
   - Profession/work type
   - Income level
   - Education level
   - Top interests
   - Likes and dislikes
   - How do audience members feel about the topic?

5. Seek to address one or more of the seven basic desires of all people:
   - To belong
   - To be respected
   - To be liked
   - To be safe
   - To succeed
   - To find romance
   - To be inspired

6. Determine the level of response you seek from your audience members:
   - Stage 1: Buy In
   - Stage 2: Approval
   - Stage 3: Action

# CHAPTER FIVE

# IDENTIFYING PROJECT RESOURCES

NOW THAT YOU HAVE ESTABLISHED the objectives of your message, it's time to actually develop the presentation. Remember, the objective of the team approach is to make certain you always have the best possible information and that you maximize all technological resources. Over a decade of presentation development, my team and I have created and refined the 3-D Outline™—a powerful tool to help you build a dynamic speech. The 3-D Outline™ can be used in a variety of ways, and it provides a simple, quick means of identifying and quantifying a great deal of information in a small amount of space. When the 3-D Outline™ is complete, it provides a detailed overview of a project or presentation.

The 3-D Outline™ is essentially a table with several columns that forces you to examine the development of your presentation from every angle. It helps you identify resources and organize your message, and ultimately it helps you determine how your message will be presented.

## The 3-D Outline™

**Presentation Title:** _____

**Date of Presentation:** _____

**Location:** _____

**Audience Size:** _____

**Audience Profile:** _____

**Presentation Objectives:**

- _____
- _____
- _____

### PRESENTATION DEVELOPMENT TEAM

**Team Coordinator** _____

**Content Specialist** _____

**Graphics and Multimedia Coordinator** _____

**Speechwriter/Presentation Creator** _____

**Coach** _____

| Item # | Time | What | Why | How | Who | Where |
|--------|------|------|-----|-----|-----|-------|
|        |      |      |     |     |     |       |
|        |      |      |     |     |     |       |

Your Team Coordinator or Project Manager is the logical person to control and maintain this document. Remember, you will draw on many resources to prepare your message, but your primary resource will be your presentation team. These team members will then identify any specialized resources necessary for creating your presentation.

You will recall that in Chapter 2 we suggested five basic positions on your presentation team, and we briefly discussed their roles. In this chapter, we will look more closely at the functions of each position.

> "Small projects need much more help than great."
>
> **D A N T E**

## YOUR TEAM

**TEAM COORDINATOR.** This person is the general manager of your presentation team. You may elect to hold this position yourself or delegate the position to a trusted, qualified associate. You may want to use different people in this role for different speeches. This person has responsibility for managing the overall preparation of your message and for coordinating the activities of all other team members. I recommend your Team Coordinator use the 3-D Outline™ as the central point of communication for the team.

The Team Coordinator must consider several key factors:

1. What type of presentation is being prepared (e.g., influence, information, inspiration)?
2. What are the presentation objectives, as determined by the funneling process?
3. Who are the audience members and what are their expectations? What kind of presentation will have the greatest impact on this audience?
4. How much time is available for developing the presentation? How much time is allotted for the presentation itself?
5. What is the venue for the presentation?

The Team Coordinator assigns other team members to conduct research and bring back information that you and the Team Coordinator can consider for the presentation. Team members should be specifically directed to find information and select technologies that will best fit the objectives of the presentation.

**CONTENT SPECIALIST.** This person should have a good working knowledge of your organization, as well as good people skills. The Team Coordinator will brief this person about the presentation and direct him or her to find the best information for consideration. The briefing should include:

1. Presentation objectives
2. Audience make up
3. Specific material that has already been identified for inclusion in the presentation
4. Length of presentation
5. Any specific research material/sources that may be helpful

After being briefed, the Content Specialist should consult with all appropriate departments within your organization to obtain the best information for the presentation and collate it for your consideration.

**GRAPHICS AND MULTIMEDIA COORDINATOR.** This position should be filled with someone who has a technical understanding of cutting-edge presentation technology and the technical capabilities of your company. The Team Coordinator and the Content Specialist should brief this person together and provide guidance on the type of atmosphere, mood, and delivery method believed to be best suited for the particular

> "'What is the use of a book,' thought Alice, 'without pictures or conversations?'"
>
> **LEWIS CARROLL**

audience. This person needs to be given factual content that will be presented at the event (i.e., numbers and facts that lend themselves to charts and graphs). The Graphics and Multimedia Coordinator should be given the responsibility for recommending the technical devices to be used at the presentation. Once this recommendation is approved, he or she then coordinates the creation of all visual and special-effects elements, as well as their use during the presentation.

SPEECHWRITER/PRESENTATION CREATOR. Working closely with you, the Speechwriter will write your presentation script. Of course, you may choose to do this yourself, or you may even use an outside professional. The speechwriter should have access to all the information that has been collected and assembled by the Team Coordinator, the Content Specialist, and the Graphics and Multimedia Coordinator.

PRESENTATION COACH. The coach pulls together all of the creative elements into a unified and dynamic whole. You might use him or her to supplement the efforts of other team members. In some cases, you might want the coach to be the Team Coordinator. Your coach should have some knowledge about every ingredient in your presentation and be qualified to back up or double check the efforts of the rest of the team. He helps fine-tune the content and technical aspects of the presentation and rehearses your delivery with you.

Below is a sample scenario to help you see how this process works.

## THE SCENARIO

As the CEO of a technology firm, you have negotiated the acquisition of a smaller company whose operations will be merged with yours within the year. Tentative agreement has been reached, and the final documents are scheduled to be signed within thirty days. There have been rumors circulating in your company about the acquisition, and many of them have been negative. There has been speculation of downsizing, and your people are nervous. Morale and productivity have been impacted. You decide you need to address your current management team to give them a factual overview of the acquisition, reverse the negative rumors, and build some excitement about the benefits of the acquisition. The company you are acquiring has a product that will fill an important market niche for your firm, and you believe the acquisition will trigger significant growth that can be sustained for many years. You want to address your management group in fourteen days. Approximately 200 people will attend your presentation. Audience members will include senior executives, middle managers, and department heads.

In the interest of time, you decide to perform the Team Coordinator role and also intend to write the speech when you have all the information you need. You select a Content Coordinator, a Graphics and Multimedia Coordinator, and your coach to work with you on the presentation development team. You must first identify the resources you need for the presentation. The 3-D Outline™ will be used to manage the project and serve as a work tool for the team members.

The number of action items can be increased as necessary, and many additional people can be added if required. Let's walk through each component of the outline and discuss them in more detail:

# The 3-D Outline™

**Presentation Title:** Undetermined
**Start Date:** May 1
**Date of Presentation:** May 15

**Presentation Location:** Undetermined
**Audience Size:** 200
**Audience Profile:** Executives and Managers
**Presentation Type:** Informational/Motivational

**Presentation Objectives:**
- To provide information about acquisition
- To calm fears related to acquisition
- To create excitement and optimism about acquisition

### PRESENTATION DEVELOPMENT TEAM
**Team Coordinator:** YOU
**Content Specialist:** Mary Lookout
**Graphics and Multimedia Coordinator:** Bob Whiz
**Writer:** YOU
**Coach:** Tony Jeary

| WHAT | WHY | HOW | WHO | WHERE |
|---|---|---|---|---|
| **ITEM 1—MAY 2-5** | | | | |
| Collect information on market niche we want to cover | To make the case for moving into this new area of business | 1. Talk to key department heads 2. Do limited market research | Mary | 1. Our Sales Dept. to verify product gap and quantify the need 2. Technical publications for product statistics and facts 3. *Wall Street Journal* archives for related information |
| **ITEM 2—MAY 2-5** | | | | |
| Collect information on company being acquired | To explain the value of making the acquisition | Interviews and research | Mary | 1. Collect financial information on firm from Accounting Dept. |

| WHAT | WHY | HOW | WHO | WHERE |
|------|-----|-----|-----|-------|
| | | | | 2. Review company's marketing materials and message<br>3. Get list of their primary customers from Legal Dept. |
| **ITEM 3—MAY 2-5** | | | | |
| Collect information on location and equipment options for presentation | To insure everything needed is available and the location is suitable | Interviews and personal expertise | Bob | 1. Coordinate with Mary Lookout on types of information to be presented<br>2. Create list of presentation aids and tools that are appropriate for presentation |
| **ITEM 4—MAY 9-13** | | | | |
| Prepare presentation | So it can be delivered | 1. Review available data<br>2. Create outline<br>3. Write speech<br>4. Prepare visual aids | You<br>Mary<br>Bob<br>Tony | CEO Conference room. Work schedule to be determined later |
| **ITEM 5—MAY 14** | | | | |
| Rehearse presentation | To ensure professional delivery | Work with presentation coach until presentation is satisfactory | You<br>Tony | At location to be determined |

## Logistics and Objectives

In the top four boxes of the outline, we have placed the logistical information that relates to the presentation, as well as the objectives that have been identified. This provides basic information at a glance for any member of the presentation team.

**Columns**

There are three primary columns in the 3-D Outline™. The cumulative effect of each column requires you to think through each step at a fairly detailed level. Let's take a look at the information that has been placed in this example.

*Item #1.* Since you plan to give the presentation in only two weeks, this entire project has a relatively short fuse. The first item covers the collection of information related to the market niche you hope to fill by acquiring the new company. You need this information to make the case to your management team for moving into this new area of business. The information you need can probably be obtained from within your organization and by doing a limited amount of research. Your Content Coordinator will perform this action item. She (Mary Lookout) will have discussions with the department heads she believes can provide pertinent data. The sample we created sends her to the sales department, but there may be other people in your company equally able to help. The Content Coordinator must have a good understanding of your entire organization. Mary may know of several places where she can turn to find the kind of information you need.

*Item #2.* The task is to collect information on the company you are buying. You no doubt have a lot of information at your disposal that was acquired in the process of buying the firm. Mary can get whatever she needs by interviewing you and other key players in the acquisition process. She can also do some market research.

*Item #3.* This item puts your Graphics and Multimedia Coordinator (Bob Whiz) to work. Bob will talk to you and Mary to determine the kind of information you intend to present. Can you benefit from using charts and graphs? What kind of atmosphere do you want to establish? Bob will combine his expertise with what he learns from Mary and make recommendations about how the presentation should be made from a technical standpoint. After his recommendations are approved, he will make sure all visuals are created and all presentation equipment is put into place.

*Item # 4.* Preparation of the speech will involve you and the entire team. The collected information will be reviewed, and the appropriate data will be selected. Since you have elected to be the writer, you will create the outline and write the speech. Note that we have included your coach (Tony Jeary) in this step. Tony will also review everything that has been done by the team and help you build the best presentation possible. Since the creation of the presentation is one of the most critical steps in the team process, we will discuss it in greater depth in the next chapter.

*Item # 5.* When the speech has been written and all the visual aids have been put in place, it's time for you to prepare yourself for delivering the speech. You and your coach will sequester yourselves and practice the presentation until it's perfect! You will refine your voice inflection and body language and become thoroughly familiar with the technical tools you will be using. Your coach will critique *every* aspect of your delivery and provide specific instructions that will help you improve your stage presence and speech delivery.

# VERY IMPORTANT POINTS

1. The objective of the team approach is to make certain you always have the best possible information and that you maximize all technological resources.

2. The 3-D Outline™ can be used in a variety of ways, and it provides a simple, quick means of identifying and quantifying a great deal of information in a small amount of space.

3. When the 3-D Outline™ is complete, it provides a detailed overview of a project or presentation.

4. The 3-D Outline™ is essentially a table with several columns that forces you to examine the development of your presentation from every angle.

5. We suggest five basic positions on your presentation team:
   - Team Coordinator—the general manager of your team who coordinates all team activities
   - Content Specialist—the person who obtains the best information for your presentation and collates it for your consideration
   - Graphics and Multimedia Coordinator—the person who oversees the creation and execution of visuals and special-effects elements
   - Speechwriter/Presentation Creator—the person who works closely with you to write the presentation script
   - Presentation Coach—the person who pulls together all creative elements into a unified and dynamic whole

6. Direct your presentation team . . .
   - To determine the type of presentation you need to make
   - To clarify your presentation objectives
   - To identify the audience types and their expectations
   - To determine the time available
   - To obtain vital information about the presentation venue

7. Practice, practice, practice. Rehearse, rehearse, rehearse, rehearse.

# CHAPTER SIX

# CREATING
# THE SPEECH

YOUR TEAM HAS ASSEMBLED THE INFORMATION you need, and now it is time to actually prepare the speech. Just as you used the 3-D Outline™ to identify your resources, you will also use it to develop your presentation. To give you a vivid example of the power of this tool, I am going to use a 3-D Outline™ we developed while working with executives of a Fortune 100 company. You will quickly notice that we refer to this company simply as "the company," and that we have generalized some of the information so as not to betray our relationship with this client.

> "You can't build a
> reputation on what
> you are going to do."
>
> **HENRY FORD**

Like most major corporations, this client sends several of its executives to major colleges and universities every year to recruit top talent. The client wanted to standardize its corporate presentation to ensure that the same message was delivered to every audience. Rather than assemble an internal presentation team, we were hired as an extended resource to help develop the presentation. The result was a presentation that could be given in fifteen minutes, thirty minutes or a full hour, depending on the time allotted by the university. We did this using the steps and procedures discussed in this book.

First, we used the funneling process (Chapter 4) to identify the objectives of the presentation. The objectives were:

1. To create enthusiasm for the company among top college recruits

2. To inspire top college recruits to consider the company as their career first choice

The one-hour version of the presentation will be used as our example:

### On-Campus Recruiting Presentation (60) Minutes

| Objectives: | | | | |
|---|---|---|---|---|
| • To create enthusiasm for the company among top college recruits<br>• To inspire top college recruits to consider the company as their career first choice | | | | |
| # | Time | What | Why | How |
| | | | | |
| Transition: | | | | |

The columns are set up as follows:

#—Each segment of the presentation will be numbered consecutively. This example presentation will have ten segments ranging from two to ten minutes in length.

TIME—The time to present each segment is placed in this column.

**What (The First "Dimension")**—This column contains a bullet summary of the information to be presented in the segment.

**Why (The Second "Dimension")**—This column establishes the reason this segment is being presented. This is a very important column, because it forces the presenter to think through the relevance of each element of the presentation.

**How (The Third "Dimension")**—This column lists the technical support and presentation tools that will be used in the segment when the presentation is being given.

**Transition**—At the end of each segment there is a transitional statement to move the presentation to the next segment.

Let's take a look at the first segment of the outline we created for this presentation:

### On-Campus Recruiting Presentation (60) Minutes

| Objectives: |
|---|
| • To create enthusiasm for the company among top college recruits |
| • To inspire top college recruits to consider the company as their career first choice |

| # | Time | What | Why | How |
|---|------|------|-----|-----|
| 1 | 3 minutes | Walk- in Welcome & Intro<br>• Welcome<br>• Personal intro and experience with the company<br>• Agenda | To welcome audience to the presentation<br>To let recruits know who you are, why you are here, and what you will talk about. To relate your personal experience with the company | Running video: Ad collage<br><br>PPT 1 on screen<br><br>Present / PPT 2-3 Olympics theme music |

Transition: Before we begin, let's see how familiar everyone is with our company . . .

As you can see, Segment One will last three minutes and all elements of the segment can be quickly viewed by the presenter.

This particular segment sets a warm tone as the speaker gives his personal statement about his career with the company. This "testimonial" personalizes the presentation and gives the speaker credibility. The "why" column focuses on the desired effect of this segment on the audience. The final "how" column provides a snapshot overview of what the audience will be seeing and hearing: a mix of video, PowerPoint slides, and audio. Finally, the transition language to the next segment of the presentation is given.

> "Few people think more than two or three times a year; I have made an international reputation for myself by thinking once or twice a week."
>
> **GEORGE BERNARD SHAW**

Let's look at the second segment:

| # | Time | What | Why | How |
|---|------|------|-----|-----|
| 2 | 5 minutes | History Quiz<br>• Ask: How many have visited this website?<br>• Review 5–6 questions pulled from website | To gain audience involvement and create interest in the company<br>To communicate the rich heritage and the many innovations and accomplishments of the company | • Show homepage slide<br>• Audience quiz<br>• Interactivity (show of hands)<br>• Prizes |
| Transition: These were just a few interesting facts about us. Now lets take a look at our company today and why we believe you should consider a career with us . . . | | | | |

The second segment lasts five minutes and involves the audience in company accomplishments. It provides a comfortable way to promote the company's many innovations and increases audience identification with the company. Then the transition moves the presentation smoothly to the next segment.

| # | Time | What | Why | How |
|---|------|------|-----|-----|
| 3 | 5 minutes | Today: A world leader<br>• History of global leadership<br>• Global brands<br>• Diversified divisions<br>• Worldwide locations<br>• people involved globally | To provide an overview of history and some of the key factors that describe us as a global business leader<br>To get recruits thinking about all the opportunity (including global) that awaits them with a diversified and thriving industry leader | Present / PPT 4<br><br>Present / PPT 5 |

Transition: As the world's largest industrial corporation, managing all the systems and processes required in product development, engineering, finance, and manufacturing, to name just a few areas, requires an enormous effort. However, to be a leader, we can't just manage them. We're out to change and improve them everyday . . .

The third segment is a five-minute overview of the company. It presents a brief history and then dramatically positions the company as a global leader. This segment ensures that the audience is aware of the worldwide career opportunities available to employees. It completes the general orientation information, and the transition statement moves the presentation to more specific areas of audience interest.

| # | Time | What | Why | How |
|---|------|------|-----|-----|
| 4 | 10 minutes | What is Functional Management?<br>• Leading force behind process improvement<br>• Combines Process & IT<br>• Diversity in career choices | To introduce and describe what Functional Management is | Present / PPT 6 |

| | | Process Framework <br> • Improvement Projects <br> • Reengineering Projects | To describe the process function of FM and relate actual projects and personal experience that may be of interest to candidates | Present / PPT 7 <br><br><br> Present / PPT 8 |

Transition: No other organization, public or private, has more computing power. As an IT professional on our team, you will have full access to these resources . . . Vast resources, diverse and challenging areas of interest, information technology mean having the opportunity to choose from all that an $800 million business can offer . . .

I'm sure you can see at this point how the 3-D Outline™ is put together and the incredible overview it gives the presenter. The segments have just the right amount of detail to make this a functional document for the presenter, yet the verbiage is simply stated and quickly grasped. Here are the final six segments:

| # | Time | What | Why | How |
|---|------|------|-----|-----|
| 5 | 8 minutes | Information Technology <br> • IT—the central nervous system <br> • Diverse technologies <br> • Challenges | To provide an overview of the IT function, pervasive applications and opportunities | Present / PPT 9 <br><br><br> Present / PPT 10 |

Transition: With these high expectations, growing needs and competitive pressures, we're challenged to be the best every day. That's why we are visiting our nation's top college IT programs for the best talent available to lead us into the 21st century. That's why we're talking to you today . . .

| # | Time | What | Why | How |
|---|------|------|-----|-----|
| 6 | 10 minutes | Looking for Leaders <br> • Process and Technology | To provide candidates with an understanding of the | Present / PPT 11 <br> Present / PPT 12 <br> Present / PPT 13 |

| | | | • Solutions Delivery | roles and | Present / PPT 14 |
| | | | • Technical Services | requirements of positions in the 3 main focus areas of Functional Management | |

Transition: We know it takes a lot to attract the best. To be sure that we do, we've developed one of the most innovative, flexible and effective career track programs for recent college graduates. We want to ensure that you match your skills and aspirations to the right opportunity— and your career path experience is stimulating and rewarding. That's why we created the College Graduate Program . . .

| # | Time | What | Why | How |
|---|------|------|-----|-----|
| 7 | 10 minutes | College Graduate Program<br>• Introduction<br>• Purpose<br>• Candidate Requirements<br>• How it works— during & after | To introduce candidates to the College Graduate Program and provide them with an understanding of what they will experience in the program, especially the rotation (exposure) and variety of exciting choices (opportunity)<br><br>To relate personal experiences with the program and its merits | Present /PPT 15<br><br>Present /PPT 16–17<br>Present / PPT 18<br>Present / PPT 19 |

Transition: We also want you to get off to the right start, and we do everything possible to ensure that you're prepared . . .

| # | Time | What | Why | How |
|---|------|------|-----|-----|
| 8 | 5 minutes | New Employee Orientation<br>• Gaining a broad view<br>• Technical Education Program | To let recruits know there is a highly structured orientation program and activities in which they will participate with other recruits | Present / PPT 20 |

Transition: When you join us, you'll visit our World Headquarters . . .

| # | Time | What | Why | How |
|---|------|------|-----|-----|
| 9 | 2 minutes | The Region<br>• Attractive, affordable communities<br>• Recreation<br>• Best schools | To convey a positive, attractive image of living in the region | Present / PPT 21 |

Transition: This part of the country is a great place to live and work—there are many benefits. The company offers great benefits, too . . .

| # | Time | What | Why | How |
|---|------|------|-----|-----|
| 10 | 2 minutes | Summary / Close<br>• Call to Action | To provide an overview of the many benefits the company has to offer, especially in comparison to other firms with initial higher starting salaries<br>To thank candidates for their consideration and encourage them to take the next step to joining our Functional Management team | Present /PPT 22–23<br><br>(music) |
| Total time: 60 minutes | | | | |

When the 3-D Outline™ is completed, the presenter has a complete, detailed overview of the entire presentation. Every content and technical-support element of the presentation is available at a glance. The speechmaker knows the number of segments in the speech, the points that will be made in each segment, why the segment is being included, the technical aids that will be used, and how to transition from one concept to the next. In my opinion after a decade of using this approach with dozens of clients, there simply is no better way to organize and prepare a presentation.

# VERY IMPORTANT POINTS

1. Use the funneling process (Chapter 4) to quickly identify clear, written objectives.

2. Use the 3-D Outline™ to create the details of your presentation.
   - *Time*—Budget the total time of the presentation.
   - *What* (The First Dimension)—Create a bullet list of the information to be presented in each segment.
   - *Why* (The Second Dimension)—Establish the reason each segment is being presented. (This is very important because it forces the presenter to think through the relevance of each segment.)
   - *How* (The Third Dimension)—List the technical support and presentation tools that will be used when the presentation is being given.
   - *Transition*—Create a transitional statement that will smoothly move the presentation to the next segment.

3. When the 3-D Outline™ is completed, the presenter has a complete, detailed overview of the entire presentation.

# CHAPTER SEVEN

# PEOPLE

THE AUDIENCE AT VIRTUALLY any executive presentation includes several groups of people: audience members; event hosts and organizers; members of the media; and, in many cases, people from "the general public." This chapter discusses in greater depth the needs and expectations of three major groups of people and how you can make a positive impact on them.

We have already talked at length about the importance of knowing your audience. Because audience members comprise the most important group, you need to consider in advance their special characteristics and how to specifically address their needs.

## THE AUDIENCE

Although most speechmakers readily acknowledge that they *should* consider the audience profile in preparing their speeches, an amazing number do not appear to do so. I have witnessed some dreadful presentations in which the content of the message totally missed the intended audience. The speaker was more focused on himself and what he was doing and saying than on the audience. The speech may have been written by a qualified speechwriter using wonderful words, but there was no connection made with the audience.

"The nice thing about egotists is that they don't talk about other people."

LUCILLE S. HARPER

The key to connecting with your audience is to thoroughly understand them. Who are these people you will be addressing? What are their concerns? What are their needs and desires that you can fill with your presentation?

When I work with executives as their personal presentation coach, I am careful to walk them through the process of identifying their audiences. On one occasion, after discussing an upcoming presentation with the CEO of a large corporation, we determined that his audience would contain four groups of people: shareholders, employees, Wall Street analysts, and members of the media. With such a diverse group, the content of the presentation had to be carefully crafted and organized to connect with all four groups simultaneously.

One way to understand your audience is to take the time to meet some of them in advance. This may take some extra effort, but the rewards and benefits can be enormous. I realize that such a practice might not be possible in all venues; but, when feasible, it's a great technique. When I make presentations, I always meet

and talk to some of the people who will be in my audience. I learn first-hand what they would like to hear and what they believe the relevance of my presentation might be to them personally and to the organization.

> The key to connecting with your audience is to thoroughly understand them.

When you are visiting with people before the presentation, try to find someone you can reference in your speech. Remember the person's name and determine where he or she will be sitting. This is a powerful technique to help your audience relate to you personally. It may not be possible for you to do this because of time constraints, but your team should be able to do it on your behalf and pass the information to you before you speak.

I have learned over the years that people attending presentations arrive with one of ten "character" identities.

## CHARACTER IDENTITIES

1. *Fast Freddie.* This is the extrovert. He wants your speech to go quickly so he can get back to doing some of the talking himself.

2. *Methodical Mary.* She thinks about things very carefully before she does them. She listens closely to the presenter to determine what course of action she should take in response.

3. *Detail Dan.* He likes to write down everything and loves the lists and charts you may use in your presentation.

4. *Friendly Fran.* She loves people and is the opposite of Detail Dan. She had rather chitchat with those around her and may very well do so during your presentation.

5. *Greg the Graduate.* He is the know-it-all and considers himself to be an expert on all you have to say. He may as well be sitting in the room wearing a mortarboard.

6. *Prisoner Pete.* He is the guy who does not want to be at the presentation, and he has his arms crossed in a "pouting defense" posture.

7. *Student Steve.* He has a pen in hand, has his lap desk out, and is taking notes. He has come to learn and is really listening to the speaker.

8. *Vacation Virginia.* She is the person sipping a pineapple drink with an umbrella in it, and she is just happy to be there instead of working.

9. *Champion Charlotte.* She is the cheerleader for the speaker's ideas and will stand up and give testimony as to why she believes in the concepts. She can validate your statements with personal experience, no matter what they are.

10. *Sniper Sid.* He is the guy who intends to shoot down your ideas no matter what they are.

> One way to understand your audience is to take the time to meet some of them in advance.

Some people may embody more than one character identity. For example, Sniper Sid and Prisoner Pete may be one and the same person. Detail Dan and Student Steve may be combined. These general character profiles are likely to exist in any group of twenty or more people. Know that these "people" are in attendance, and plan and deliver accordingly.

## AUDIENCE CHECKLIST

Here is a short checklist to help you analyze information about your audience:

- Create a profile of the average audience member, including age, background, marital status, education, income and job type.
- Create a list of people your audience members would probably admire. This will give you great insight into their attitudes.
- Talk with people who have attended similar presentations in the past.
- Talk with other executives who have made presentations to similar groups of people. Find out what went well and what bombed.
- Interview the event planner to get his or her perspective on the audience.
- Request a list of likely attendees, and then pre-poll them by calling them in advance to see what they expect. (Your team can do this for you.)

> "There is no point at which you can say, 'Well, I'm successful now. I might as well take a nap.'"
>
> **CARRIE FISHER**

The more thorough you are, the more solid the foundation you have for your presentation.

## PERSONALITY TYPES

Audience members also reflect varying personality types. I like to use the D.I.S.C. personality profile in evaluating audience members. My good friend, Dr. Robert Rohm, and I wrote a book on this subject, *Presenting with Style*, which discusses in detail how to present to each personality type.

Every person on earth will fall into one of these four categories. Tests can be administered to determine where individual

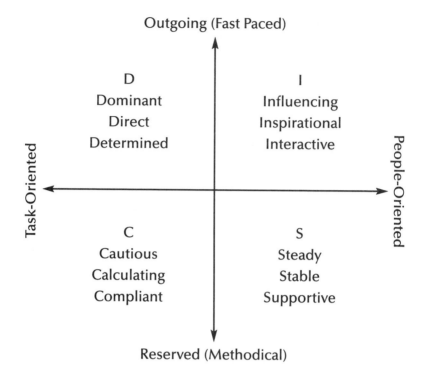

people fall within the categories, but enough research has been done to enable us to identify where specific groups of people fall as well.

*"D" Personalities.* Company presidents, CEO's, and strong leaders usually have "D" personalities. They want to get to the bottom line of things in a hurry! "D" types don't want to be involved in long, touchy-feely conversations. They want to kill the cow, skin it, and eat it as quickly as possible. Obviously, if you are addressing a group of "D" personalities, you don't want to waste a lot of time getting to the core of your message.

*"I" Personalities.* These are the people who love to talk . . . and talk . . . and talk, . . . and they never meet a person they don't like. "I" personalities tend to become sales people, trainers, or speakers, or they enter other careers that allow them an opportunity to spend most of their time with people. "I"

personalities want to feel good about themselves, and they don't want a lot of bad news or too much detail. If you are addressing a group of "I" types, you need to get them involved with you. They love to participate, and they will gladly do anything you ask them to do . . . as long as it's fun and exciting.

*"S" Personalities.* These people are sympathetic to the needs of others and have a high degree of empathy. Counselors and people who love to teach have "S" personalities. An "S" personality will gladly make personal sacrifices to help another person in need. If you suspect you are addressing a group of "S" types, let them know how they can help. They will be anxious to do so.

*"C" Personalities.* These people want to know all the nitty-gritty details, and they are willing to spend as long as it takes to get them. Accountants, auditors and investigators have "C" personalities. If you are addressing a roomful of "C" types, bring a lot of charts, graphs and statistics. The "C" personality wants to know the tasks that lie ahead and each step necessary to accomplish those tasks.

> "Economists are people who work with numbers but don't have the personality to be accountants."
>
> **ANONYMOUS**

The twist to this is the fact that people can't be defined as being solely a "D," an "I," an "S" or a "C". We all have mixtures of these traits that blend together in varying degrees to produce our own unique personalities. However, one of these four characteristics will usually be dominant. You may be primarily a "D" personality but have a lot of empathy with others—in other words, you have "S" qualities mixed with your dominant "D" characteristics. Simple tests are available that can determine the exact mix of your personality traits. (Your training department probably has information on this subject if you are interested in learning more.)

The challenge for you as a speaker is twofold. First, determine the *overall* characteristic of your audience and adjust your content and delivery style appropriately. Second, avoid the tendency to present information the way *you* would like to receive it. If you are a "D" personality, you will naturally tend to present things like your "D" personality dictates—straight to the point with bottom-line conclusions. Remind yourself frequently that everyone is different and that others process information in ways that may seem foreign to you.

## CONNECT EARLY

It is critical that you connect with your audience early in the presentation, and your understanding of the audience is the key to making this connection. There are several ways you can do this:

- Arrive early. By arriving before your audience, you send the message that you care enough to get things ready in advance.
- Meet and greet the audience yourself. I never cease to be amazed by presenters who stand off in one corner reading notes while the audience files in. Get on your feet and greet! This is a great opportunity to build rapport. Ask people their names, shake their hands, and make good, solid eye contact. Ask them some personal questions, and let them know you are interested in them. I suggest you do this even if you are about to speak to 10,000 people. You can have your team invite some random members from the audience backstage if it's not possible to mix with the entire audience.

> "My play was a complete success. The audience was a failure."
>
> **ASHLEIGH BRILLIANT**

- Grab their attention quickly. You should get your audience involved in the first three minutes of the presentation. There are three things audience members love, and you can get their attention right away if you give all three to them quickly. First, they want you to *respect* their time, their dignity and their feelings. Second, they want *rapport* with you. You can establish this by sharing common ground. You may want to open with a statement that is aimed at reducing the "nervousness" of the audience. (When executives speak, audiences tend to have a higher level of anxiety than when lower-level employees speak.) Third, they want you to *entertain* them in some way. Bring some humor or a fascinating personal story that the audience will appreciate. You might want to show a funny video clip or even read a funny story. For more ideas, I suggest my book, *Speaking Spice: 201 Stories to Entertain and Inspire*, co-authored with my associate John Davis. If you can deliver these three things in the first three minutes, you will establish a strong connection with your audience.

> "The best audience is intelligent, well educated, and a little drunk."
>
> ALBEN W. BARKLEY, U.S. VICE PRESIDENT

- Let them know what's in it for them. Convince them that they aren't wasting their time.
- Make *eye* contact. Search out a few friendly faces—especially focus on those who are smiling, nodding and laughing at your jokes. You draw power by making eye contact, and a good place to start is with the people on the front row. My rule is to hold eye contact for *several* seconds to assure that the person knows you are connecting. This works even in a large room where you can't really see

anyone; you must hold for several seconds in a particular direction, even if you don't have eye contact.

- Show genuine enthusiasm. Let your audience know you're happy to be there.

## EVENT HOSTS AND PROGRAM CHAIRPERSONS

Event hosts and program chairpersons are very important to an event's success. These people don't need a lot from you, but what they do need is significant. Remember, event hosts and program chairs may have been working for weeks or months to successfully organize and produce the event. When the day of the event arrives, the two most nervous groups are the core speakers and the program organizers. You both want the event to be a success, and neither of you wants any last-minute surprises or disasters.

> "Do you think I could buy back my introduction to you?"
>
> GROUCHO MARX

Your presentation team can help the program hosts by providing them with a few simple things *well in advance* of the event. One item that frequently gets pushed to the last minute is a good introduction of the speaker for the program chairperson to use. I believe introductions are extremely important; and if they are prepared properly, they can significantly enhance the incoming acceptance level of the speaker.

Think about some of the speaker introductions you have heard in the past. Do any of them stand out in your memory? Probably not. Introductions are usually treated as routine exercises that are rather bland. They usually consist of a resume of the speaker's accomplishments and a statement of how happy the group is to have the speaker there to address them. This approach may accomplish the need of having an introduction, but it doesn't *enhance* the message you will give the audience that day. I believe a good introduction should do precisely that. This won't happen if you merely provide a stock introduction. Take a more creative approach.

Here are some of the elements I recommend you include in your introduction:

1. WHO YOU ARE AND WHAT YOU'VE ACCOMPLISHED. This is what most introductions usually provide. Don't stop there. This part of the introduction is necessary, but it should not be the entire message.

2. IDENTIFY WITH THE GROUP. The introduction should tell in simple, concise "overview" terms why you have come to address the group and why the information you will share is important to them. This can be stated in a couple of sentences to "hook" the audience members and peak their interests.

3. PREVIEW THE SPEECH. A brief peek at one point you are going to make can spark interest.

4. ASK FOR APPLAUSE. The announcer should enthusiastically lead the audience in applause as you are welcomed to the microphone or lectern. This will loosen up the room and get your audience warmed up for you.

A custom introduction should be prepared by your team for every presentation you give. Your written introduction should be provided to the program hosts days or even weeks in advance of your talk so the introducer can prepare his delivery and so the information you provide can be incorporated into promotional materials.

The program chairperson/host might find a copy of your 3-D Outline™ to be helpful. Or you can use the outline format to address specific questions the host may have about the time you will require and the technical support you will need. I also recommend that you give the event planners a separate, detailed list of the equipment you will need to display your visual aids. The best scenario is for one of your team members to spend time with the program host to discuss all the details of your speech and answer any questions he or she may have.

## THE MEDIA

In many instances there will be reporters and cameras at your presentation to report what you are going to say. If you believe the event has the potential to attract media attention, I suggest you find out in advance what members of the media will be there. Then you need to help them understand your message before they hear it. You no doubt have had a lot of experience dealing with the media, and I realize you likely have many media information tools at your disposal. Let me simply remind you of the basic resources.

> "Television: A medium. So called because it is neither rare nor well done."
>
> **ERNIE KOVACS**

The primary, traditional communication package for the media is a professional press kit. The press kit should include your biographical information, information about your organization, and any number of other items that have significance. What your standard press kit may not currently contain is information about your specific presentation or speech. Your press kit should include a synopsis of what you will be saying and a summary of the major points in your speech. In some cases, you may want to provide the complete written text of your remarks. I also suggest that you anticipate questions the reporters may have and answer them in advance in a question/answer section *in your press kit*. This information accomplishes two goals. First, it helps the reporter organize his report; and second, it helps you control the impact of your message on the general public.

As you know, the risk of any media-covered event is the "spin" the media outlet may put on your message. I believe you need to do everything in your power to help a reporter and his editors interpret your message the way you desire for it to be interpreted. If you anticipate potential problems because you are dealing with sensitive information, provide all of the factual data you can to explain or alleviate concerns. As a general rule, there is no substitute for the truth. When dealing with the media, you must be prudent but candid. The media is cynical and looks for deception. The worst thing you can do is give reporters a reason to mistrust you or cast suspicion on your company.

# VERY IMPORTANT POINTS

1. At virtually any executive presentation, the audience includes several groups of people:
   - Audience members
   - Event hosts and organizers
   - Members of the media
   - In many cases, people from "the general public"

2. Although most speechmakers readily acknowledge that they *should* consider the audience profile in preparing their speeches, an amazing number do not.
   - Recognize audience "character" identities:

     Fast Freddie—wants your speech to go quickly so he can talk himself

     Methodical Mary—listens closely to determine her response

     Detail Dan—loves the lists and charts

     Friendly Fran— will likely chitchat during your presentation

     Greg the Graduate—the know-it-all

     Prisoner Pete—does not want to be present

     Student Steve—has come to learn

     Vacation Virginia—happy to be doing anything other than working

     Champion Charlotte—the cheerleader who can always validate your statements with personal experience

     Sniper Sid—will shoot down your ideas no matter what they are
   - Recognize audience personality types (D.I.S.C.), and adjust your content and delivery style appropriately.
   - Meet them in advance to learn more about them and personalize your message.

3. The key to connecting with your audience is to thoroughly understand them.

4. There are three things audience members love, and you can get their attention right away if you give all three to them quickly:
   - Respect of their time
   - Rapport with you
   - Entertainment

5. It is critical that you connect with your audience early in the presentation, and your understanding of the audience is the key to making this connection.

6. Help the event hosts help you by writing your own introduction:
   - Tell who you are and what you have accomplished
   - Identify yourself with the audience
   - Preview a segment of the speech
   - Request that the host ask for applause

7. Be ready for the media
   - Determine who will attend
   - Provide press kits
   - Help the media "spin" your message in your favor
   - Be prudent but candid

8. The more thorough you are, the more solid the foundation you have for your presentation.

# CHAPTER EIGHT

# PLACES AND THINGS

L ET'S ASSUME YOUR SPEECH IS prepared and the day is approaching when you will deliver it. Don't fall into the subtle trap of thinking that the hard part is over. You also have to consider the place (environment) where you will be speaking and the tools you will be using as you deliver your message. This chapter briefly examines the various speaking environments and provides tips on how to manage them.

You may not be aware of the unique challenges that various venues present to a speaker. Our focus will be on how to employ your team to help you maximize the presentation potential of each facility. This involves understanding the physical layout and the best way to interact with an audience in each venue.

## FACILITIES

There are six major types of facilities for executive presentations:

1. Auditoriums
2. Stadiums
3. Convention centers
4. Hotel ball rooms
5. Media rooms
6. Internal, corporate facilities

Each venue has advantages and limitations. Your challenge as an executive is to direct your team to maximize the advantages and circumvent or fully compensate for the limitations. The following chart summarizes major considerations you and your team should keep in mind when evaluating a facility.

| Factor | Sample Considerations |
|---|---|
| GROUP SIZE | Meeting rooms should not be too large or too small; if you have to err on one side; slightly too small is often better than rattling around in wide-open spaces. If you are faced with a space that is too large, bring people together in one end or corner of the room. |
| LOCATION | Your audience members may not be happy campers if you make them drive or fly to a place that is viewed as inconvenient or "too far." |
| INTERACTION | Often, interaction between the speaker and participants is difficult with groups of 25 or more people. Careful layout selection and use of roving microphones can mitigate this difficulty for some kinds of speeches. |

**CONTROL** The degree of control for the speaker varies widely based on the layout of the room and group size, and generally is inverse to interaction. If you are dealing with controversial or difficult subject matter, choose an environment in which you can maintain control and limit interaction.

**POWER** Power balance among participants can be significantly impacted by layout and seating. For example, if VIP's or members of the media are to attend a very large event, you may want to provide special seating arrangements so you know where to direct eye contact at appropriate times in your speech.

**MEDIA** Visual media (slide presentations, videos, overheads, flip charts) all come with limitations relative to sight lines and sight distances. A common (and often major) error in presentations involves the use of media that can't be seen by many attendees.

Sound systems are critical. Your message is hindered if people cannot hear you or understand your words clearly.

Lighting is also very important. If there is a spotlight in your eyes, you may not be able to see your script or teleprompter, or anyone in the audience. Spots can also add years to your age and make you look ill if the colors are not right.

**PRIVACY AND NOISE** "The walls have ears" is a good watchword in many facilities. If you're dealing with sensitive or confidential material, find a place with good isolation.

Similarly, if you want your group to concentrate on what you are saying, you can't be in a room next door to a loud celebration or backed up to a busy kitchen.

AVAILABILITY    Sometimes you will be forced to speak in a venue that has been selected by others or is the only one available. In my experience, these "sites" have included warehouses, tents, factories, parking lots, and city parks. The skilled speaker must be flexible enough to work around almost any environmental inhibitor if there is no better spot available. It is really important that you *look at the facility well in advance* and use a checklist such as the one on the next page to determine your specific plans.

"It takes more than three weeks to prepare a good impromptu speech."

MARK TWAIN

The general information you need about each type of facility is essentially the same, but the specifics change from facility to facility. Even venues of the same type will differ. Just because you understand the layout and functionality of one auditorium doesn't mean you understand *all* auditoriums.

## FACILITIES CHECKLIST

Following is a comprehensive list of things you need to know about a facility:

This is a fairly comprehensive facility checklist. If your team diligently collects this information, you should have no facility-related surprises awaiting you on the day of the event.

## EQUIPMENT

You may wish to use various tools in the delivery of your presentation. When your team reviews the facility well in advance of the date of the presentation, it should also determine the availability of equipment at the site and any options or restrictions that may impact your plans.

> "Knowledge is of two kinds. We know a subject ourselves, or we know where we can find information on it."
>
> **SAMUEL JOHNSON**

I recommend that my clients create an event book for *every* presentation they make. The book should contain all of your 3-D Outlines™ and all other checklists related to the event. Make sure your presentation team members "sign off" on facility and equipment checklists and that all details related to the facility and equipment are double checked within twenty-four hours of the event.

| Item of Consideration | Questions to answer - information to collect | Why the Information is needed |
|---|---|---|
| Audience Seating Layout | 1. What kind of facility is it?<br>2. How is the audience seating arranged?<br>3. Can the seating arrangements be adjusted, or are the seats permanent?<br>4. Will the audience be comfortable or cramped during your talk? How big are the seats? | An understanding about how the facility seating is arranged will help you plan possible interaction with the audience and give you an advance preview of what you will see from your speaking location. |

5. Will audience members be able to take notes comfortably?

6. Does every audience member have a clear view of the stage?

7. How far away is the most distant seat from the stage?

8. Are audience members in front of the stage close enough for good eye contact?

| | | |
|---|---|---|
| Audience Seating Capacity | 1. How many seats does the facility have?<br><br>2. How many of the seats will be occupied at your presentation? | Being aware of the seating capacity of the facility and the size of the expected crowd will help you prepare for what you will face as a speaker and what the audience will be able to see, hear, and "feel" in the environment. |
| Communication Facilities | 1. Are communication facilities available?<br><br>2. What communication services are available?<br><br>3. What fees are charged for services? | The availability of communication facilities may help you overcome a last minute challenge. |
| Exits | 1. Where are exits to the stage located?<br><br>2. Where are exits to the building located? | When the speech is over, you need to know where and how to exit the stage and the building. |

| Facility Floor Plans | Obtain a copy of the facility floor plan. | Most facilities have floor plans, and having one in advance will help you find your way through the facility more efficiently. |
|---|---|---|
| Green Room Availability | 1. Does the facility have a "green room?" <br> 2. Where is it located? <br> 3. What is available in the room? | Green rooms are rooms designated for waiting and final preparation prior to your appearance on the stage. |
| Heating and A/C Systems | 1. Does the facility have heat and air conditioning? <br> 2. What is the expected temperature at the facility on the day of the event? | You need to plan your attire so you will be comfortable during your presentation and not perspire. |
| Labor Available | 1. Is labor available to assist in moving equipment and props? <br> 2. Is union labor required? <br> 3. How are arrangements made to use available labor? | If you have props or equipment to use, some facilities require it to be handled by union laborers and charge a fee for doing so. |
| Lighting | 1. What kind of stage lighting is used at the facility? <br> 2. Will spotlights be used? <br> 3. Can text be read easily at the podium? <br> 4. Is the audience area illuminated? | You don't want to walk on the stage and be hit with lights you weren't expecting. Understanding the lighting situation in advance is very helpful in knowing what you and the audience will be able to see. |

| | | |
|---|---|---|
| Loading & Unloading | 1. Does the facility have a designated loading/unloading area or dock?<br>2. Where should props and equipment be delivered, if necessary? | Many facilities are under union contracts that have specific requirements regarding deliveries and material movement inside the building. |
| Media Rooms | 1. Does the facility have a media room?<br>2. Where is it located?<br>3. How is it configured?<br>4. Will a press conference be held after the speech? | If there is a media room for the press, you should know where it is and how it is configured. |
| Mounting the Stage or Speaking Area | 1. Where will speakers approach the stage?<br>2. Where will speakers enter the stage?<br>3. Will stairs be climbed? If so, how many?<br>4. Can the audience see speakers climbing the stairs?<br>5. Are ramps employed on the stage? If so, where? | You must be aware of how you are expected to enter the stage when you are introduced. |
| Parking and Traffic Routing | 1. What are the normal traffic routes and patterns at the facility?<br>3. Will traffic patterns be changed on the day of the event?<br>4. Is reserved parking available for speakers? | Being aware of special traffic routes or parking requirements can save you time and avoid wasteful delays. |

|  | 5. Is reserved parking available for the speaker's staff?<br>6. What kind of parking is available (covered or uncovered)? |  |
|---|---|---|
| Press Location | 1. Will the press be covering the event?<br>2. If so, where will reporters be seated?<br>3. What media will be present?<br>4. Will TV/video cameras be in operation? | If the press is covering your event, being aware of how they are seated can help you "work them" more effectively. |
| Reception Areas | 1. Will there be a reception area?<br>2. Where is it located?<br>3. How is it equipped?<br>4. Is food service /catering available? | You may want to hold a reception before or after the event, or you may be asked to attend a reception sponsored by the meeting hosts or sponsors. |
| Seating for Speakers | 1. Is there a designated seating area for speakers?<br>2. How far is it from the stage?<br>3. How many people will be seated in the area? | You should be aware of where you will be seated and with whom before you are introduced. |
| Security | 1. Does the facility provide parking lot security? If so, what kind?<br>2. Does the facility have a written security policy? If so, acquire a copy.<br>3. Does the facility use metal detectors? | Large facilities frequently have stringent security requirements. Be aware of these to avoid delay or embarrassment. |

|  | 4. Will security personnel be present during the presentation? |  |
|--|--|--|
|  | 5. How can security personnel be contacted in case of an emergency? |  |
| Sight Lines | 1. Can the speaker see the entire audience from the podium? | You need to know what you will see from the podium and how well the audience will be able to see you. |
|  | 3. Are there places on the stage where audience visibility is restricted? |  |
|  | 4. Will the speaker or audience view be restricted by TV cameras, teleprompters or other equipment? |  |
| Sound Systems | 1. What kind of sound system exists at the facility? | You should use the microphone best for you, and you should know your options. |
|  | 2. Will stage monitors be used? |  |
|  | 3. Can speakers bring their own microphones? |  |
|  | 4. Can the facility sound system accommodate the desired microphones? |  |
| Stages | 1. How large is the stage at the facility? | There may be physical characteristics of the stage that limit movement or prop displays and impact the way you have to deliver your speech. |
|  | 3. What type of stage is it? |  |
|  | 4. Will the entire stage be utilized? |  |

| Item of Consideration | Questions to Answer/ Information to Collect | Why the Information is Needed |
|---|---|---|
| | 5. Will other people be on the stage during the presentation? 6. What equipment will be on the stage during the presentation? | |
| VIP Seating | 1. Is there an area designated for VIP seating? 3. How many people can be seated in the area? 4. Where is the area located? | If VIP's are present, you will need to know where they are in case you want to acknowledge them. |

| Item of Consideration | Questions to Answer/ Information to Collect | Why the Information is Needed |
|---|---|---|
| Audio Visual Equipment | 1. What equipment is necessary to deliver the presentation? 2. What equipment is available at the facility? 3. Is there a charge or fee for using facility equipment? 4. Can speakers bring their own equipment? 5. Are there any special equipment restrictions imposed by the facility? | The equipment you use for your presentation is critical. You should plan the use of it well in advance of the event. |
| Display devices | 1. What display devices are needed to deliver the presentation? | |

|  | 3. Is a jumbo screen available? <br> 4. Are TV monitors in the facility? If so, where are they located and how many are there? | The equipment you use for your presentation is critical. You should plan the use of it well in advance of the event. |
|---|---|---|
| Microphones | 1. What type of microphone is preferred by the speaker (e.g., headset, lapel, hand-held)? <br> 2. Is the desired microphone type available at the facility? <br> 3. Are backup microphones available? | |
| Operators | 1. Are equipment operators available to assist the speaker (slides, computer, etc)? <br> 2. What type of instruction do operators need prior to the event? <br> 3. Can speakers bring their own operators? <br> 4. How can advance rehearsal be accomplished? | |
| Podiums and Lecterns | 1. What type of podium or lectern is needed for the presentation? <br> 2. Is the podium or lectern available? <br> 3. Is the podium or | |

| | lectern the right height? (KEY: adjust podium height without the use of a step to give the executive maximum height) | The equipment you use for your presentation is critical. You should plan the use of it well in advance of the event. |
|---|---|---|
| Props | 1. Are props planned for use during the presentation?<br>2. Are there physical restrictions that impact or impede prop use? | |
| Recording devices | 1. Are recording devices available for use?<br>2. What types of recordings can be made?<br>3. What are fees and charges for equipment use? | |
| Remote equipment operating capabilities | 1. Will remotely operated devices be needed for the presentation?<br>2. What types of devices are needed?<br>3. Does the facility have these devices available? | |
| Slides and their operation | 1. Are slides to be used during the presentation?<br>2. Who will operate the slide show equipment?<br>3. What instruction/ training is needed? | |

| | | |
|---|---|---|
| Teleprompters | 1. Will a teleprompter be needed for the speech? How many prompters?<br>3. Is a teleprompter available?<br>4. Who is in charge of coordinating teleprompter use? | The equipment you use for your presentation is critical. You should plan the use of it well in advance of the event. |
| TV Cameras | 1. Will TV cameras be in use?<br>2. Where will they be positioned?<br>3. What is the purpose of the cameras?<br>4. Who is operating the cameras? | |
| Side Table | 1. Is a side table available to hold a glass of water, props, awards or other items? | |

## Helpful Hints from the Experts

### Graphics

- Keep it simple, whatever it is (i.e., text, charts).
- Use pictures to illustrate your point.
- Try not to use clipart—it does not look professional.
- If you are using a production company, *trust* the people who are helping you—that's what they do for a living.
- Everyone has time constraints, but a presentation is much more powerful if some thought is given to it. A presentation thrown together at the last minute generally looks it.
- Try not to be overly literal with your graphics—a little imagination goes a long way!

—CAROLINE PHEFFER, GRAPHIC ARTIST

### Teleprompters

- Decide ahead of time which of the three teleprompting formats you will use:
    Bullet points
    Loosely scripted (most difficult)
    Completed scripted
- Sit with the teleprompter operator in person ahead of time to format spacing and the layout of the script on the screen in order to coordinate pacing.
- When choosing font size, remember—the larger the font, the fewer words per line and the less thought content visible on the screen.
- If possible, do an "off-line" rehearsal in a small rehearsal room before the event. This allows for an intimate formatting and/or editing session with the operator. If you only rehearse on the main stage, contact with the operator is limited.
- Make it *conversational* (customized to the executive's style and word choice). Be willing to rehearse!

—LEON HANSON, TELEPROMPTER OPERATOR

# VERY IMPORTANT POINTS

1. Employ your team to help you maximize the presentation potential of each facility. Six common types of facilities you may encounter:
   - Auditoriums
   - Stadiums
   - Convention centers
   - Hotel ball rooms
   - Media rooms
   - Internal, corporate facilities

2. Use a facilities checklist to learn as much as you can about your speaking venue. Key factors you need to know about each facility:
   - Size
   - Location
   - Interaction possibilities with audience
   - Control
   - Power
   - Media
   - Privacy and noise
   - Availability

   If your team diligently collects this information, you should have no facility-related surprises awaiting you on the day of the event.

3. The equipment you use for your presentation is critical. You should plan the use of it well in advance of the event. Use an equipment checklist to determine:
   - Things you will need to deliver your speech
   - The division of labor between your staff and the venue staff

4. Keep an "event book" for every presentation. The book should contain all of your 3-D Outlines™ and all other checklists related to the event.

# CHAPTER NINE

# MATERIAL

THINK BACK TO A TIME YOU HEARD a speech that really hooked you. What made it so good? My guess is that the speaker made a connection with you on a personal level in two critical ways: he captured your mind intellectually and established empathy with you emotionally. To capture intellect, a speech must be logically constructed and challenge thought processes. To capture the emotions, a speech should contain material with which the audience can identify personally. Nothing seems to establish empathy better than the inclusion of good stories, interesting quotes, practical examples, and a smattering of appropriate humor. These things bring a personal touch to every speech

> To capture the emotions, a speech should contain material with which the audience can identify personally.

and make the information you are delivering more believable and personally applicable.

Previously, I discussed the various types of messages that are presented in speeches. To refresh your memory, let's look at three of the four types again:

1. MESSAGES OF INFLUENCE. A message of influence is aimed at convincing people of something in a way that motivates them and causes a change in their behavior. You may want your employees to adopt new methods. You may want consumers to buy your products or services. There are many subjects of influence, but they all involve motivating an audience to some kind of action.

2. MESSAGES OF INFORMATION AND EDUCATION. Informational messages are designed to increase knowledge or improve the skills of audience members. An educational presentation involves explaining concepts and principles. The use of graphics and visual tools tends to be extensive in these kinds of presentations.

3. MESSAGES OF INSPIRATION. An inspirational message may have one of several different objectives. You may want to instill new attitudes. You may be trying to inspire your audience to recharge morale or boost productivity. A successful inspirational message always taps the emotions, and the use of real-life stories is very effective.

> "There were so many stories around, it was almost inevitable some of them would turn out to be true."
>
> NIGEL EVANS

Anecdotal stories and real-world examples are the most effective means to energize all three types of messages and help you accomplish your speech objectives. Your challenge is to find the stories and examples that will effectively amplify your presentation. To determine which stories those might be, you need to understand the defining characteristics of an effective story.

## GOOD STORIES

Stories "work" for specific reasons. There are four basic elements:

1. *Good stories are about real people.* Fictional stories are not as effective as real-life stories, because the "trust" factor of a fictitious story is much lower. People are far more interested in the experiences of *real* people. Human beings identify with other human beings. If the story is told skillfully, the listener should be able to place himself in the story or achieve a sense of knowing the subject of the story in an almost personal way. A great technique is to obtain a real story from someone in the audience with whom you are talking before your presentation, and then use it during your speech.

2. *Good stories involve real-world situations.* Stories that deal with fabricated situations are also more difficult for listeners to accept. If you attempt to present a fabricated analogy as true and the audience discovers this deception, it can cast doubt on the validity of everything else you say. Real-world stories can't be disputed! If a real-world story is told well, the listener will be able to immerse him or herself in the dialog and vicariously experience the event as the speaker tells it.

A great technique is to obtain a real story from someone in the audience with whom you are talking before your presentation, and then use it during your speech.

3. *Good stories have a unique, surprise ending.* Stories that have great endings keep a listener on the edge of his seat during the entire presentation. Perhaps the best example of a speaker that uses this technique is the famed newscaster Paul Harvey. In his "The Rest of the Story" broadcasts, each story shares a common format. He begins by telling about a person, using only his first name or nickname, and tells

some interesting and entertaining facts about his life. He presents the person as a normal, everyday person; but at some point in the story, the person does something special. At the very end of the story, Mr. Harvey finally reveals the full identity of the person. The "John" in the story might turn out to be John F. Kennedy or John D. Rockefeller. The surprise ending always brings the story to a powerful conclusion that is increasingly anticipated with eagerness as the story unfolds.

4. *Good stories are positive in nature*. If you want to lose your audience, start your speech by telling a string of stories with bad endings. Negative stories depress people, and they don't want to hear them. There are times when negative pieces of information may need to be presented; but if that is the case, the negative information should be balanced by a positive story involving what *can* occur if certain remedial or problem-solving steps are taken. Generally speaking, positive stories have a much stronger impact than negative stories. This is particularly true when you are trying to convince a group of people to do what you want them to do. When you have a choice between positive and negative, choose a story with a positive outcome.

> "The wisdom of the wise and the experience of the ages are perpetuated by quotations."
>
> **BENJAMIN DISRAELI**

## MATCHING GOOD STORIES WITH YOUR OBJECTIVE

Be certain the story you choose is compatible with the type of message you are seeking to convey. The first step is to determine the kind of message the story will illustrate and support.

MESSAGES OF INFORMATION. Speeches that are designed to provide information need a story or example that will validate both the truthfulness and the significance of that information. Rarely is a speech limited to merely providing information. You might think of the informational part of a presentation as the bait you will use to catch your fish. For your overall message to be effective, your audience must *believe* you. Using stories that validate the importance and accuracy of your information is one way to enhance the credibility of your entire presentation.

For example, if you are providing information about a new product you are introducing, tell stories that will demonstrate that product's quality and effectiveness. You might acquire the names of the people in your company responsible for the product's development and tell the story of its creation from their perspective. Telling the story of the hours spent, the personal vision, and the dedication of your employees enhances the factual information about the product.

> Always seek to "personalize" information and make the information relevant for each audience member.

Always seek to "personalize" information and make the information relevant for each audience member. Look for stories of people who have benefited from the product or service and give sufficient details regarding their positive experiences.

**MESSAGES OF INFLUENCE.** When you are attempting to influence people, you must compel them to accept the *truth* of what you are saying. Your goal is to have them adopt your opinion, your perspective, your view. You need stories about people who benefited from a change of opinion or an enlarged perspective.

My friend Zig Ziglar is a master at delivering messages of influence, and his presentations are rich with stories that bolster the validity of the information he presents. For example, when Zig is trying to convince people of the importance of setting goals, he tells stories about people who changed from being non-goal-setters to active, enthusiastic goal-setters. He tells what their lives were like before they started setting goals and what happened to them after they started setting goals. Success stories of people who have taken action on the message you are sending are the best sto-

> "After all, all he did was string together a lot of old, well-known quotations."
>
> **HENRY LOUIS MENCKEN**
> on Shakespeare

ries you can use to validate the truth of your message and influence your audience.

MESSAGES OF INSPIRATION. Inspirational messages are incredibly suited for special stories that ignite enthusiasm in an audience. Look for true stories of real people who became inspired and took action. Tell stories about dreams that became true. Tell about the struggles of a dreamer who turned his or her vision into a successful reality. When people hear what others like themselves have been able to do, they are inspired!

## HOW TO GET THE RIGHT STORIES

The good news is that good stories are readily available. They are all around you! The bad news is that you may not have been looking for them and consequently missed most of them. More good news is that you can start looking for them today!

I strongly recommend that every top executive build a private file of stories, quotes, and examples that can serve as a powerful arsenal of support for his or her presentations. If you have not collected this kind of material in the past, you will be shocked at the volume of information that is available once you start looking for it. The key to building this powerful arsenal of examples is to create a routine system that allows you to collect the information continually.

The first step is to establish that every piece of information you place in your "story file" must fit into one or more of the three types of messages we have discussed: influence, information or inspiration. As the files grow, you may find other categories helpful, but begin with these three.

The second step is to identify where stories can be found. Several prime sources for stories and quotes are:

THE INTERNET. The sheer volume of information available through the Internet is overwhelming, but a person who knows how to search and find information can mine mighty veins of it with specific value for his or her presentations.

NEWS SOURCES. Newspapers and magazines routinely feature stories about real people in real-life situations. All you must do is clip these stories and file them appropriately.

CUSTOMER LETTERS. Your company no doubt receives letters from customers who give positive testimonials about your products or services. Duplicate and file the best of these for your use.

INDUSTRY PUBLICATIONS. Your company is probably subscribing to many publications unique to your industry or professional field. These publications often have stories and information you can use.

TOP PERFORMERS. Your company has people who are consistent top performers and very successful. Each of these people has a unique story that can be told and they are often very inspirational. Seek them out. Write them up.

CLASSIC STORIES OF HISTORY. Thousands of people throughout the centuries have accomplished great things and led highly inspirational lives. Identify your favorite people in history and study their lives.

These are some of the most obvious places to discover the stories you need. As you establish your filing system and a method for routinely collecting stories, you will discover many additional sources yourself. When you begin to *look*, you will begin to *see*!

The third step of finding the right stories is to designate or recruit people to assist you in the collection and collating processes:

THE PRESENTATION TEAM. Make the members of your presentation team aware of the basic principles discussed in this chapter and point them toward the sources where stories can be found. Direct your team to engage in the ongoing acquisition of good story material and to pursue stories for specific presentations.

ADMINISTRATIVE ASSISTANTS. Your administrative assistant may know more about your needs than you do! Ask him or her to help you build your collection of stories.

OTHER EXECUTIVES. Your executive peers are likely to be voracious readers. Let them know that you collect certain types of stories and ask them to clip good stories for you as they encounter them.

YOUR SPOUSE. Spouses can be a great help in identifying stories. They are likely to be pleased that they were asked to help!

GENERAL CONVERSATION. Ask other people about stories they may have to share with you. Professional speakers are always on the alert for a good story they can use and are not shy about asking other people to share the best stories they have heard.

CLIPPING SERVICES. Professional clipping services can be hired to locate specific types of information from publications all over the world. If you want to jump start your system and collect a lot of information in a hurry, this approach may work well for you.

## OTHER TYPES OF MATERIALS

In addition to stories, other types of materials can be used effectively in speeches and presentations:

CARTOONS. I often see presenters successfully use material from cartoons such as "Dilbert" (Scott Adams) and Salt & Pepper (*Wall Street Journal*) to inject humor into their presentations. I personally keep a file with "favorite cartoons" that cover most subjects and that can be used for most occasions. A word of caution: Use cartoons sparingly; and be certain to obtain proper permission for their use if your remarks are going to be taped or published, or if you intend to use the cartoon repeatedly.

TV COMMERCIALS. TV spots are designed to get attention and deliver a concise message fast. People like to see both "old favorites" and new ones that have not yet been broadcast. You might consider commercials featuring your own company, as well as those of other firms.

"HERITAGE" AND "IMAGE" VIDEOS. These are not intended to be humorous, although they may contain humor. Such videos can provide a concise view of the origin of your company, an overview of its historical accomplishments, a look at your company today, or a glimpse into the future of your company.

PICTURES AND VISUALS. The old adage, "one picture is worth a thousand words," is still true today. Visuals of real customers using your products can be powerful credibility bolsters. Pretty pictures can set a mood. Simplified graphic models can be used to illustrate complex concepts.

STORIES VIA VIDEO. Purposefully produced clips with visuals and sound bites of customers, dealers, shareholders, or employees can be effective in supporting your main points.

**MUSIC.** Carefully selected music can set the tone for your speech and help strengthen the overall theme or objective of your message. For example, if you are trying to get people "up" for a major challenge, use music such as the *Rocky* or *Chariots of Fire* themes. Rock and roll, classical, country and western, and other genres also have well-known themes that inspire and motivate. A musicologist, such as my friend Al Lucia, co-author of *Rock Your Way to Happiness,* should be considered as you put together your team for any major presentation. You can visit Al's web sites, www.jukeboxlearning.com and www.allucia.com, to learn more. Again, use care to avoid copyright infringement. Information about obtaining licenses is available on Al's web sites or at www.ASCAP.com.

I cannot overstate the importance of using stories, quotes, and examples to give *power* to a message. However, there are also other ways to get your audience involved with you. Ask audience members to stand up, write down key points, or repeat a key phrase to the person sitting next to them. You can use props, present skits, role-play a scene, or show a funny video clip created by your PR Department. Build an arsenal of presentational material to inform, persuade, and inspire virtually any audience you face!

---

As a final note to this arsenal concept, my company, High Performance Resources, has created a unique "Speaker's Arsenal Box." This resource has been provided to some of my top executive clients as an added value to my coaching relationship. It contains hanging files on 25 core subjects, each containing highlights of books I have studied that pertain to that particular subject. This resource is designed to serve as a basic tool and can easily be expanded. Contact us if you have an interest in this unique tool.

---

# VERY IMPORTANT POINTS

1. To capture the emotions, a speech should contain material with which the audience can identify personally.

2. There are three common types of executive presentations:
   - Messages of Influence
   - Messages of Information and Education
   - Messages of Inspiration

3. Include good stories in your speech. Choose stores that:
   - Are about real people
   - Involve real-world situations
   - Have a powerful ending with a unique twist
   - Are positive instead of negative

4. Match stories to your speech objectives.

5. Stories should be compatible with the overall emotional tone of your message.

6. Personalize stories and make them relevant to your audience.

7. Every top executive should build a private file of stories, quotes, and examples that can serve as a powerful arsenal of support for his or her presentations. Sources for these tools include:
   - The Internet
   - News sources and feature magazines
   - Customer letters
   - Industry publications
   - Top performers
   - Classic stories from history

8. Other materials to consider including in your speaker's arsenal:
   - Cartoons
   - TV commercials
   - Heritage and image videos
   - Pictures and visuals
   - Stories and quotes presented on video
   - Music
   - Testimonial letters
   - Surveys
   - Important articles
   - Quotes

# CHAPTER TEN

# PREPARATION AND PRACTICE

THE MORE PREPARED YOU ARE, the more spontaneous you can be! The best speeches and presentations have a relaxed, natural flow to their delivery. It's almost as if the presenters are somehow creating the speeches in their minds as they speak. A perfect example of this is Dr. Martin Luther King's "I Have a Dream" speech. As he stood framed in the portals of the Lincoln Memorial, Dr. King sounded as if he were pouring out the deepest concerns of his heart for the first time. The audience marveled as it listened to a perfectly worded and extremely well crafted speech that felt so spontaneous.

> "The more prepared you are, the more spontaneous you can be!"
>
> **BOB GEROLD**

That day in Washington, D.C., was not the first time Dr. King had expressed the "I Have a Dream" concept. The fact is, Dr. King had delivered that same speech many, many times in churches and other meeting halls across the nation. The speech was so well prepared and practiced that Dr. King could deliver it in a spontaneous way. It is that *feel* of spontaneity I believe we should all strive to achieve when we deliver our speeches, and the key to such spontaneity is preparation and practice, practice, practice.

The personal characteristic that creates a spontaneous feel is confidence. When a person is confident, he appears natural and relaxed. He knows what he is going to say and how he is going to say it. He can then be "in the moment"—keenly aware of the communication bridge he is building with his audience. That "in the moment" connection is perceived as spontaneity.

## REASONS TO PRACTICE

Let's assume that you have your speech objectives finely honed. You've located and included the best content possible and couched it in the best possible language. Every section of your presentation has been thoroughly crafted. You have all the data you need about the facility. All the necessary equipment has been arranged. From a technical perspective, you're ready to hit the ball out of the park. There's only one hurdle left. You have not yet *delivered* your presentation, even in a practice session.

"Practice is the best of all instructors."

**PUBLILIUS SYRUS**

In my experiences with many top executives and major corporations, I have yet to encounter a major project that did not require some tweaking. Adjustments are always necessary when reality and theory come together. The actual doing of things creates little situations that somehow escape the planning process. Corrections must be made in the "real time" of delivery. Words and phrases may need to be adjusted for smoother enunciation, words that accompany visuals may need to be edited, and the sequence of some ideas may need to be altered.

You face an executive decision. You can choose to discover these problems in a practice setting, or you can discover them on the day of your presentation in front of a live audience.

You will discover a number of things when you rehearse your speech. You likely will discover some strengths in the presentation that were not obvious at the planning stage, and you will no doubt discover weaknesses that were concealed.

> "In theory, there is no difference between theory and practice. In practice there is."
>
> **YOGI BERRA**

Identifying strengths and weaknesses in a practice environment enables you to build on the strengths and eliminate the weaknesses. Rehearsal allows you to convert unknown factors into known factors.

## GETTING STARTED

Most people find it awkward to talk to themselves. Unfortunately, that's the way your preparation and practice should begin. There are two phases to practice. The first phase is a solo performance, and the second phase is a full dress rehearsal that involves others.

Phase One has five steps that should be completed before you schedule a full dress rehearsal. These steps can be done alone, but you can invite others to work with you if their presence makes you more comfortable—this is just a matter of personal preference.

1. *Mentally rehearse the outline.* Get a copy of the 3-D Outline™ you prepared for your presentation. Read it over and over again until you have all of the elements of the presentation established in your memory. Make mental notes of each section. Note the elapsed time of each section and make sure you have a clear understanding about the objectives of each section (the why's). Look at the technical tools that will be used to enhance each section, and be sure you have a good understanding about how and when they will be displayed. Make sure the slides, overheads, charts, and video clips will send the messages they are intended to send and will match what you are saying at the time they are displayed. When you are comfortable that you have "visualized" your presentation from beginning to end, you are ready for the next step.

2. *Anticipate different audience responses.* Now that you have internalized the outline, go back through it again and visualize the audience in the facility where you will be speaking. Try to imagine what it will be like to give your speech and try to imagine how the audience will react to each segment of your presentation. Where will they laugh? Which points of the presentation are the most serious? How will the audience respond to those points? Are there elements you can add that will strengthen your message?

> Imagine how the audience will react to each segment of your presentation.

3. *Rehearse your presentation verbally.* Now it's time to start talking. Get out your 3-D Outline™ and a copy of the text of your speech. If you are using cue cards in lieu of a complete text, get your cue cards. Find a quiet place where you can be

alone without interruptions. Read the entire presentation aloud from beginning to end. As you read the speech or work through your cue cards, use a red pencil to mark where you sense any awkwardness in your delivery. Don't stop reading as you make the marks. Try to take a "snapshot" of the parts of the presentation that need work.

Immediately read through your speech a second time. See if you experience the same awkwardness at the points where you made red marks. If so, stop and make a note about what you think the problem may be. Tweak each area that has a red mark if it continues to be a problem. Repeat this process until you are satisfied with the flow and feel of the words. Recite your speech as many times as necessary to achieve the feeling of spontaneity you want. Replace any words you find awkward or those over which you tend to stumble.

4. *Record the speech.* After you are comfortable with the flow of the speech, record your speech so you can hear yourself. Any type of recorder is satisfactory to use at this point. Just make sure the length of the tape is adequate to record your entire speech. As you listen to your speech, read the text or cue cards. Keep your red pencil handy; and as you listen to the tape, mark any places that appear to sound rough or unnatural. Record your delivery of the rough spots again and again until you are satisfied with them. When you are satisfied with your delivery of the entire presentation, you are ready for the final step of Phase One.

> Recite your speech as many times as necessary to achieve the feeling of spontaneity you want.

5. *Present the speech to another person.* Find one, two, or more people to come in and listen to your verbal delivery. Provide them with copies of your text or your cue cards and ask them to read along as you deliver the presentation. Tell them

you want them to listen for the tonality of your voice, because approximately forty percent of a presentation's impact is driven by the voice tones of the speaker. Ask your mini-audience to evaluate:

- How well your words and transitions work together
- How comfortable you appear to be with the material
- How your posture, pronunciation and word speed work together
- How you can improve the presentation.

Remember, what sounds good on paper and even in your head doesn't always work in front of other people. Any problem is simple enough to fix if a friend, spouse, coworker, or coach catches it in advance of your real presentation. Practicing in front of people also gets you through the process of moving from solo mental practice to a live dress rehearsal, which is Phase Two of preparation and practice.

> The tonality of your voice represents approximately forty percent of your presentation's impact.

## THE DRESS REHEARSAL

If you have used the services of a professional coach on your presentation team, you already know the great benefits of having an objective expert involved in the development of your speech. The rehearsal phase of your preparation is one of the key times when the input from a coach can make a highly significant difference between what is acceptable and what is extraordinary. It is at the dress rehearsal that the coach brings the totality of your presentation to the "highly polished" level and brings your level of confidence to its apex. Because I believe so strongly in the benefit of using a professional coach,

I want to discuss the dress rehearsal phase as if I were working with you personally. I will tell you what I do for my clients, and you can use this information as a benchmark for making your own decisions about whether to have a coach and about how to organize your own dress rehearsal.

> The input from a coach can make a highly significant difference between what is acceptable and what is extraordinary.

If your presentation team has functioned properly, it has achieved the following:

1. Determined your speech objectives, using the funneling process
2. Created the actual presentation
3. Developed specific demographics on your audience
4. Obtained advance information about the facilities and equipment you will use

The dress rehearsal is the event that brings their efforts together, and the coach is the person that "tests" the entire presentation package. I like to think I provide a form of "quality insurance" for those executives who hire me. I review every detail of every piece of work that has been done in advance of the dress rehearsal and make sure the best approach has been taken for every segment of the presentation. I check the list of slides, overheads, or video clips that will be used and make sure the equipment is appropriate. I meet with the meeting producer (if there is one) and go over all of the logistical details of the presentation. Basically, any item that might be of concern or worry to you, the speaker, is checked and double-checked to ensure things will happen the way you expect them to happen.

The actual dress rehearsal is the key preparation event. I set up a room as close in design as possible to the room where the actual presentation will occur. My team helps me replicate the room, including the location of furniture and props that will be present on the stage. This gives you a real sense of the space you will have and gives you a working familiarity with each piece of equipment.

Creating the proper environment for the dress rehearsal is very important. Executives often fly in to our Presenter's Laboratory near Dallas, Texas. This studio laboratory has been constructed especially for the purpose of coaching top leaders individually and privately. The facility includes a professional stage and provides state-of-the-art technical equipment to accommodate any type of presentation. We have built-in video capability that allows us to tape the rehearsal and then use it as part of the coaching session.

> "I cannot teach anybody anything; I can only make them think."
>
> SOCRATES

Regardless of the facility you use for your dress rehearsal, it is important that you deliver the presentation as closely as possible to the way you plan to do so on the day of the event. If you are rehearsing on your own without a professional coach, all of the people who will be assisting you during your presentation should be present at the rehearsal: your speechwriter, PR people, event producer, teleprompter operator, and projectionists.

As you begin your dress rehearsal, videotape your speech as you deliver it. As a presentation coach, I observe this run-through with a critical eye and make notes of any fresh ideas I may have to help my client improve his or her delivery. After the speech is finished, I review the video with my client, step by step, pointing out weaknesses of the presentation and isolating areas that might be improved.

Expect to receive creative ideas from your coach as you practice. As I have worked with people in practice situations, I have never failed to identify several things that might be adjusted to elevate the performance of the executive or to significantly improve the creative impact of the presentation. I draw ideas from the hundreds of presentations with which I have assisted since 1983.

A dress rehearsal requires an investment of your time, but less time is required if your coach and team have planned the rehearsal in advance. When you have completed a well planned dress rehearsal, you will know exactly what to expect on the day you deliver your actual message. You will know your material, and you will be more relaxed and spontaneous in your delivery. You will

> There is no substitute for preparation and practice.

have a higher degree of confidence, because you will be totally prepared. There is no substitute for preparation and practice. A full dress rehearsal is well worth the time and effort required.

A special word needs to be added here about your wardrobe. Certain patterns in suits and ties can become optical nightmares on television or on a video. In live audience presentations, unpolished shoes can send a powerful negative message. Even the nature of dress, from full-blown formal to resort casual, needs to be considered. Test your attire with people that are representative of your audience. Purchase special clothing for the event if your own closet doesn't already house what is most appropriate.

Finally, there are a few additional types of presentations that may require a special type of rehearsal:

THE VIDEO-ONLY PRESENTATION. There may be instances where you want to create a video presentation for mass duplication and distribution. Your hand gestures and facial expressions need to be adjusted for this medium. Your wardrobe needs special attention, because you don't want a "bad hair day" or an unruly tie captured on tape forever. Remember, people focus intently on videos, and they observe more details than they do in a "live" venue.

THE VIDEO + LIVE AUDIENCE. In this scenario, you play to two audiences—the camera and the people present during the taping. You must balance the use of full body gestures (which the live audience will see) and the upper body and facial expressions that will be captured by the cameras.

THE SMALL, INTERACTIVE ROOM. This is the type of presentation that might be involved with a press conference or analyst briefing. In addition to rehearsing your prepared remarks, you should practice answering the tough questions that may be directed to you.

THE STADIUM SETTING. Your enunciation and phrasing have to be very precise/precise/precise for the echo/echo/echo in the huge space you will encounter. Poorly enunciated words or a drop in tone or volume may hamper the reception of your message.

> Man's mind stretched to a new idea never goes back to its original dimensions.
>
> **OLIVER WENDELL HOLMES, JR.**

I recommend that, if possible, you conduct your Phase Two dress rehearsal with the actual production crew scheduled for the day of your presentation—those who will cue the videos, change the slides, operate the lights, man the roving microphones, and so forth. Many otherwise well crafted presentations have been ruined by slide changers who got behind and could not catch up gracefully.

If the presentation is not in your hometown, plan to arrive in the city early and *make* time for a dress rehearsal. This may mean getting into the facility at midnight, so a nap in the afternoon is a good idea to allow you to rehearse and not be sleep-deprived at the live event.

# VERY IMPORTANT POINTS

1. Great presentations are always well rehearsed.

2. The more prepared you are, the more spontaneous you can be.

3. You will discover a number of things when you rehearse your speech. Practice and rehearsal can help identify the strengths and weaknesses of both the content and the delivery of your presentation.

4. Solo practices should involve:
   - Mentally rehearsing the presentation outline
   - Anticipating audience responses
   - Verbally rehearsing the presentation
   - Recording the speech
   - Presenting the speech to another person for feedback

5. Dress rehearsals are a must for ensuring there are no surprises on the day of the event. A dress rehearsal requires an investment of your time, but less time is required if your coach and team have planned the rehearsal in advance.
   - Use a professional coach to direct the rehearsal
   - Know your material
   - Be confident in your delivery

6. Make sure the slides, overheads, charts, and video clips will send the messages they are intended to send and will match what you are saying at the time they are displayed.

7. Expect to receive creative ideas from your coach as you practice.

8. Even the nature of dress, from full-blown formal to resort casual, needs to be considered.

9. I recommend that, if possible, you conduct your Phase Two dress rehearsal with the actual production crew scheduled for the day of your presentation.

# GO TEAM GO!

A S A SENIOR EXECUTIVE, YOU HAVE the power and authority to dramatically impact the personal and professional lives of all who are in the sphere of your influence. People listen to you with an ear for action. They expect to hear something that is noteworthy. They expect you to present an outstanding speech that hits the mark. They want you to be strong, bold and decisive. People want to believe that you know what you are doing and to feel safe in your leadership.

Take charge of your speechmaking!

Put together a team to help you make the most of every speechmaking opportunity you face.

Develop clear core objectives for each speech, using a funneling process that considers all elements related to the audience and the results you desire.

Use 3-D Outlines™ to identify your resources and requirements, and to prepare your speech. Make sure your presentation has been crafted to match both your "personality" and the "personality" of your specific audience, as well as the "environment" of your specific venue.

Check and double check to make certain that all details related to the facility and equipment have been nailed down.

Make certain your speech is enhanced with good stories about real people in real-life situations, and that these stories have a strong, positive punch line or moral point. Enhance your message with visuals that reflect your purpose and help clarify information.

And then rehearse your speech under the direction of a professional coach in a professional setting that is as close as possible to real-time delivery. Practice, practice, practice.

I have no doubt that if you take these steps, you will make a confident, professional, and dynamic impression every time you take center stage. When the day is done, your personal image and career will be strengthened, the status of your corporation will be enhanced, and specific needs within your company will have been addressed in a positive, forward-moving manner.

Those who speak from the top should be top-notch speakers!

# FINAL WORDS

The information presented in *Speaking From the Top* is designed to help the busy executive overcome many time-consuming challenges that negatively impact his/her presentations. Time is the critical element for all executives. Endless numbers of people, opportunities, and challenges are standing in line to consume their valuable time. I have learned from working with executives that one reason they have difficulty preparing for critically important presentations is that they think they have to do it all themselves. *Speaking From the Top* clearly demonstrates that there is a better, more effective way.

*Speaking From the Top* encourages each executive to create and utilize a presentation team to elevate his/her effectiveness as a communicator. Executives earn their compensation packages for a variety of reasons, but their primary value is found in their abilities to lead others to action in support of their visions and goals. Obviously, the key to creating action in others is to effectively communicate, inspire, and motivate those who must take the action.

Effective presentations are critical to your success as an executive. I urge you to take the principles, suggestions, and techniques of *Speaking From the Top* and put them into practice. I guarantee they will change your entire perspective on communication and produce results you never thought possible.

If you are considering additional help and ideas on improving your own presentation skills (even if you're already a great presenter, but want to go even higher) or if there is a need in your organization to improve these particular skills, please review the following pages. They briefly describe my company, High Performance Resources, Inc., and my personal coaching and workshop experiences. I would love to visit with you personally to discuss your particular circumstances. Give us a call (1-877-2-INSPIRE).

## I WANT YOUR HELP!

Finally, it is my sincere hope that the information presented in *Speaking From the Top* has been valuable to you. I am constantly seeking better ways to teach and train people to improve their speaking and presentation skills. I would really appreciate any comments and suggestions you have about the book. I invite you to write to me and share your thoughts. What are the best and most effective parts of the book? How could I have said things better? What could be added to make the book even more effective? You can reach me at:

High Performance Resources
8105 Firestone
Flower Mound, TX 75022
tony@hprinc.com

In addition, I have a powerful desire for this information to reach as many people as possible. Nothing is more effective than a strong recommendation from a "satisfied customer." Would you be willing to help others become more effective executives by spreading the message of *Speaking From the Top*? In the next several months, you will have the opportunity to tell many people about this book. Some of your peers and professional associates can benefit from this book, and you will be doing them a great service to tell them about it.

I hope to hear from you soon. If you write to me, I'll send you a free autographed copy of my book, *Inspire Any Audience*, so please include your return address.

At your service,

Tony Jeary—Mr. Presentation™

# FOUR OPTIONS
*from*
## TONY JEARY—MR. PRESENTATION™

# THE PRESENTER'S LABORATORY
## *A Coaching Experience*

You know...
- how valuable it is to get people inspired and have people buy in to your message and to take action when you speak
- you have some level of speaking anxiety and you would love to be extremely confident
- you could reach a higher level if you could find the RIGHT COACH

Calling all...
- Execuitves
- Sales Professionals
- Entrepreneurs
- High Achievers
- Speakers
- Celebrities

Tony Jeary—Mr. Presentation™—has perfected an incredible one-on-one, customized coaching day that will impact your success IMMEDIATELY! This power-packed immersion experience is customized for your specific needs. Tony and his staff spend the necessary time in advance, familiarizing themselves with your business; your message; your audience; your presentation style; and, of course, your objectives—so your time is maximized.

You are invited to come spend a day with Tony and his staff in his "unique studio" part of his custom home/office complex located on two beautifully landscaped acres near DFW International Airport. This setting is a result of a three-year design process to create a relaxing, productive atmosphere that stimulates creativity. You will have access to his personal library, which has been compiled over 20 years. It contains thousands of book recaps that Tony has personally compiled. It also contains hundreds of video talks from the very best speakers and executives from around the globe. It is conveniently arranged and organized to allow you to make selections as your session progresses. His friendly staff members have been with him for years and work as a team to help you build your presentations, rehearse, create an arsenal, and bring you to the next level in just a few hours. Very few people can do what he and his team can do in just a single day.

If you are unable to come to work with Tony in Dallas, he will meet you at any location around the globe. Tony is the personal speaking coach for many successful speakers, executives, and professionals. He coaches people like Morgan Matlock, Miss Dallas; Peter Lowe, success guru, who produces success seminars featuring Zig Ziglar, Brian Tracy, and many other prominent celebrities; and presidents and CEOs from Fortune 100 companies such as Ford, Wal-Mart, New York Life, Shell, Texaco, and American Airlines.

# INSPIRE ANY AUDIENCE
## *Custom Workshop "Experience"*

Six powerful workshops tailor-made for you by Tony Jeary—Mr. Presentation™

### HAPPY AUDIENCES AND HAPPY CLIENTS

Every time Tony conducts one of his customized workshops, he is swamped with letters and favorable remarks from both meeting organizers and participants.

> "Exactly what our team needed to move ahead . . ."
> "Thank you for exceeding my expectations . . ."

## CLEAR FOCUS ON YOUR OBJECTIVES INSURES RESULTS

You will be amazed at Tony's skill, experience, and ability to produce results for your team. He pours more than two decades of intensive study and real-life experience into every workshop. His amazing focus and ability to incorporate the "big picture" objectives that you have set for the event are second to none. Each workshop is customized to each particular audience and each particular organization (executive, sales, management, marketing, training).

### Speaking From the Top

Corporate Executives learn to:
- Synergize your presentation team (speechwriters to teleprompters)
- Secure audience connection and buy-in
- Save valuable preparation time
- Leverage the power of an effective presentation development team

### Inspire Any Audience

Based on Tony's best selling book. Learn how to:
- Effectively prepare and develop a presentation in half the time, using our famous 3-D Outline™
- Overcome the NERVOUS jitters
- Get 100% audience buy-in to your message

### Presenting Your Business Visually

Take advantage of and build your brand to:
- Fully leverage your graphic identity, from paid advertising to fax coversheets
- Capitalize on special event marketing

- Bring your marketing efforts to a higher level—get people calling and asking to do business with you and your organization.

## We've Got to Stop Meeting Like This

Quit wasting everyone's time. Based on Tony Jeary and George Lowe's book *We've Got to Stop Meeting Like This*:
- Know when and when not to meet
- Learn to build the right agenda
- Conduct efficient and more productive meetings

## Persuade Any Audience

Whether one-on-one or in teams of 100's, learn simple techniques that will help:
- Perfect and map your sales process
- Improve your closing ratio
- Bring consistency to your sales force
- Improve your sales presentations for greater buy-in

## Training Other People to Train

Equip your training force with new ideas to:
- Add spice to your training
- Uniquely equip your training team
- Improve your facilitation skills
- Accelerate training development that creates rave reviews for being right-on and not wasting a minute.

# SUCCESS ACCELERATION
## *A Boot Camp Experience*

Twice a year, Tony brings a small group of committed participants to his estate in the Dallas metroplex to work interactively with him in a small group. Success is accelerated by learning and applying proven principles from successful people who have gone before us. Tony has done precisely that. From more than 20 years of obsessive study and application, he has developed a one-day workshop experience that is overflowing with proven and useable principles that will expedite your way to success.

Each workshop experience is highly customized based on attendees' needs. The base of the day is comprised of four two-hour modules, each supported by one of Tony's highly acclaimed books.

## DESIGNING YOUR OWN LIFE

The journey begins even before you arrive. Using Tony's step-by-step guide, you will develop a solid foundation for building a successful life. This workbook will be further completed during the course of the workshop as we look at all the facets of the "Balance Wheel of Life"—financial, spiritual, physical, social, family, and educational. Really get to know what you want and what drives you.

## BUSINESS STRATEGIES FOR PEAK PERFORMANCE

Building upon your goals and values, we develop a concise plan for taking your business to the desired level. We work with you to identify operating strategies that support your vision. Each strategy will be assigned a set of specific, tactical actions for making your vision a reality.

## PRESENTING YOUR BUSINESS VISUALLY

Next, learn how to attract people and business your way. We review a 68-question audit to evaluate all aspects of marketing that apply to all businesses. From defining public relations and paid advertising to coordinating business cards, web sites, and fax coversheets, this exercise will show you how to maximize your marketing efforts and bring opportunities and prospects to you.

## INSPIRE ANY AUDIENCE

Finally, you will discover how to effectively present your spoken message. This module is based on Tony's best-selling book that Zig Ziglar calls "the ultimate presenter's handbook." You will learn to develop presentations in a short amount of time and delivery your message in a way that will help you sell more, work the phone better, and leverage every presentation you make—speeches, meetings, sales talks, and more.

All this in a single day! Quantum leap your success—spend a day with Tony at his unique studio!

# ACCELERATED ACHIEVEMENT™
## *Strategic Planning*

Tony Jeary has been the CEO of several multi-million-dollar companies and understands the bottom-line impact of strategic planning. In a truly unique, one-day planning session with Tony, you will accomplish results that would normally take days. Tony and the HPR team will lead you through the creation of a one-page WordZar™ Matrix for each of the following four processes for making strategic planning painless, purposeful, and extremely powerful:

**SWOT Overview Matrix**—Tony helps you build a solid foundation for your strategic plan through an intense exercise that identifies your organization's specific strengths, weaknesses, opportunities and threats.

**Strategic Plan Matrix**—You will come away with an extremely action-oriented plan and a focused set of objectives and supporting tactics. You will also identify the people in your organization responsible for executing the plan.

BRANDING PROCESS MATRIX—Tony's skillful ability to hone in on key ideas will unleash the power of branding for your organization, product, process, or personality. The questions in the branding process have been crafted to help you define what you want the market to think of your brand, the core purpose of your brand, what others think of your brand, what barriers exist for your brand, and more. The process is compounded by applying the content of the Branding Process Matrix to a critical review of an organization's current marketing collateral. The basis for this powerful exercise is Tony's simply administered 68-question audit featured in *Presenting Your Business Visually*.

PERFORMANCE STANDARDS MATRIX—Tony has mastered the ability to lead organizations in an amazingly short amount of time to craft a set of precise standards that enables the team to operate at peak performance. He couples the priorities of management and staff with the insight gained by working with thousands of organizations around the world. The result is buy-in and a common set of shared expectations for performance.

## THREE MORE REASONS FOR CHOOSING THE ACCELERATED ACHIEVEMENT APPROACH

In a single session with Tony and his team, you will take advantage of . . .

INTERNAL BENCHMARKING—Tony will help you bring your organization's best ideas to the forefront. This exercise leads to the discovery of the vast knowledge contained within individuals and corporate silos that can be of benefit to the entire organization.

EXTERNAL BENCHMARKING—Because Tony coaches executives from so many different companies, he is able to cross-pollinate "best practices" from one industry to another, which often helps jump-start a trend in a particular industry.

KNOWLEDGE ARSENAL—Tony has created this powerful tool as a result of more than two decades of dedicated and voracious study. It is a rare collection of presentation, strategic planning, and business acumen that includes thousands of book summaries, manuals, samples, and research on dozens of topics that are available to all clients at no charge.

Tony Jeary has a unique ability to blend strategy, management team synergy, organizational momentum, and corporate message into one compact whole. In fact, he has written more than a dozen books on how individuals and organizations accelerate success, including *Business Strategies for Peak Performance.*

## HIGH PERFORMANCE RESOURCES, INC.

The name says it all . . . High Performance Resources. HPR, founded by Tony Jeary, is a company defined by its ability to develop human resources into *High Performance Resources*. We are a results-oriented team focused on increasing the effectiveness of individuals and improving the performance of organizations. We are lean, fast, and different!

High Performance Resources is a unique "extended resource" company with a large network of strategic alliances representing many years of experience in providing a broad range of learning and performance-improvement services. We quickly apply proven techniques to clarify the issues, organize a comprehensive plan of action, and then follow through with the fulfillment. *We make "A" players . . . on every team!*

HPR's team of professionals is made up of renowned experts in performance, presentation, and communication skills. Through the inspired leadership of Tony Jeary, HPR's founder and CEO, we have authored an extensive library of learning and performance-improvement tools focused on inspiring both entire organizations and individuals to higher levels of performance and productivity.

HPR has committed over 20 years of collective discipline to refining our processes, library, and contacts. With over 500 initiatives in 35 countries and 14 languages, Tony Jeary and his team have amassed an incredible record of delighted and *repeat* clients.

Call us today (1-877-2HPRINC) for a free brochure on our services and to discuss your particular situation or need. Visit our website at www.MrPresentation.com. We can change people, enhance skills, and improve bottom-line results.

# OTHER RESOURCES

## WEB DESIGN

Free Advertising Synthenet Corporation, delivers superior value to its clients by assisting them to meet their business challenges by using web technology. Synthenet adds value to its clients' businesses by taking the time to understand them and the impact that the designed solution will have on their business.

Synthenet's design, development and project management services include projects that range from basic web design up to database driven web sites with a full array of interactive features, including on-line order and inventory systems.

A partial list of past and current clients include: Polaroid Corporation, PalmGear.com, ecookbooks.com, Palm Computing, Handspring, Synergy (#219 on the Inc. 500), IDG Books, Tap Magazine, etc.

You may contact them at:

367 West Main Street
Northborough, MA  01532
(508) 393-1820
www.synthenet.com

## GRAPHICS SPECIALISTS

Corporate Graphics specializes in the design, development and production of interactive communications. Helping our clients communicate more clearly using delivery tools such as the Internet other multimedia technologies is our primary focus.

In business since 1989, we currently employ a team of 32 professionals comprised of interactive designers, programmers, project managers, and Internet strategists. The tools have changed over the years, but the need remains the same: creative, solutions-based products that meet your communication objectives.

Our solid mix of creative and technical skills coupled with experience and superior customer service has earned us the privilege of working with Alamai, Cisco, Gillette, EMC, Fidelity, CMGI, and many other well-respected companies. Samples of our work and a client list are available at www.corporategraphics.com.

We would welcome the opportunity to work to speak with you about a plan to help your organization communicate effectively via thee Internet and multimedia. I will follow up, or please feel free to call me anytime.

You may contact them at:

76 Otis Street
Westborough, MA  01581
(508) 898-2500
www.corporategraphics.com

# GLOSSARY OF TERMS

## Anecdote

A short story used during a presentation to illustrate or emphasize a point.

## Arsenal

There are two kinds of arsenals in speaking—the physical arsenal and the mental arsenal. The first is a file, box, or drawer where the presenter or executive's Communication Department keeps all kinds of information for use in future presentations (i.e., testimonial letters, magazine articles, book reviews, quotes, video clips, news clips, past speech outlines). The second (the mental arsenal) is what you keep in your mind to use in your talk or spontaneously. Things to keep here are real life stories, examples, jokes or one liners, or personal happenings that can have a meaningful point.

## Articulation

Clear, concise formation of consonant and vowel sounds. Articulation results in speech that is easy for the audience to understand.

## Body Language

Mannerisms or gestures used for the purpose of emphasizing a point. Studies show that success in a presentation depends about 7% on the words spoken, 38% on the tone of the words spoken, and 55% on the body language of the speaker.

## Business Entertainment

The use of activities, games, or role playing during a presentation to counter a short attention span. Usually, these activities are placed at five- to seven-minute intervals.

## Coach

The presentation coach is a person of extreme skill and experience who can bring instant value to a client in a particular area based on his or her past experience and study.

## Conclusion

Final section of a presentation during which main concepts are summarized and reemphasized.

## Connotation

Attitude or emotion associated with a word; an overtone. (See Denotation.)

## Continuous Improvement

Commitment to using audience feedback and other forms of criticism to continually improve presentation skills.

## CPA Model

C=Content of the presentation
P=Presentation venue
A=Audience
(Most people look at the "C" and "P", but don't put sufficient focus on the "A".)

## Credibility

A speaker's believability. A credible speaker is one that has the trust and confidence of the audience.

## Deductive Reasoning

A process of reasoning that bases conclusions on a general rule. Individual examples are explained and justified by the rule. (See *Inductive Reasoning*.)

## Denotation

Literal dictionary meaning of a word; a word's definition.

## Empathic Listening

Listening that occurs when an audience identifies with a speaker and gives emotional support.

## Evaluative Listening

A type of listening that results in a decision-making process.

## Eye Contact

Making direct visual contact with members of the audience. Eye contact develops trust and credibility.

## Facilitator

One who simplifies information so that the audience can easily understand concepts and relationships. The facilitator incorporates games, role playing, and other interactive methods to involve the audience.

## Feedback

Response of audience to presentation.

## Four Audience Tensions

In every presentation, four sources of tension exist: audience to presenter, audience to environment, audience to audience, and audience to material.

## Funneling

Processing of all possible presentation material to arrive at three major objectives for the presentation.

## Identification

Ability of an audience to relate to presentation; perception that speaker is similar to them and is trustworthy.

## Impromptu Speaking

Speaking with little or no preparation and no use of notes.

## Inductive Reasoning

Process of reasoning that uses specific examples to explain a general rule.

## Informative Presentation

Seeks to expand audience knowledge by defining concepts and relationships.

## Inspire

Unique ability of a speaker to move an audience. Listeners not only hear words, but act upon them.

## Instructor

Speaker or presenter that provides information or instruction to an audience. May or may not use visual aids. May or may not use interactive methods.

## Introduction

Beginning of a presentation. Section that states purpose and provides preview of material that will be covered.

## Lecturer

Speaker or presenter that provides information to audience. Communication is generally one way.

## Participants

In an interactive presentation, the audience members are referred to as participants. The term reflects the dynamic and interactive atmosphere that a presentation seeks to create.

## Perception

Meaning given to the understanding of concepts; generally does not incorporate interactive method.

## Persuasive Presentation

Presentation that seeks to move an audience to a particular action or belief.

## Public Communication

Communication with a large group. One person speaks as an audience listens.

## Speech Communication

Sending and receiving oral messages for the purpose of creating meaning.

## Subconscious Desires

Needs or wants that nearly all of us share. They include: to belong, to be respected, to be liked, to be safe, to succeed, to find romance, to be inspired.

## Targeted Polling

Means of monitoring individual audience responses; seeking feedback from particular individuals.

## Testimonial

Endorsement of person, place, or thing. Usually, testimonials from celebrities are used.

## Verbal Survey

Method of monitoring audience response during a presentation.

## Visual Aid

Any audio or visual aid to a presentation; may include charts, maps, graphs, tapes, movies, overhead projections, slides, and flip charts.

# ABOUT THE AUTHOR

Tony Jeary's authority on public speaking is acclaimed by such gifted presenters as Zig Ziglar, Dr. Ken Blanchard, Brian Tracy, and Dr. Robert Schuller. His proven training programs and ten published books on the subject have earned him the title of Mr. Presentation™. As the president and CEO of a multi-million-dollar company, High Performance Resources, Inc., Tony delivers custom workshops for *Fortune* 500 Companies. His reputation as a premier "speaking coach" has lead him to provide personal coaching for presidents and CEOs of companies such as Shell Oil Company, Texaco, Ford Motor Company, American Airlines, New York Life, and Sam's Club.

Tony's high-energy style, paired with his unparalleled optimism, captures the attention of his audiences. His personal commitment is to equip his listeners in a matter of days—or even hours—with skills that would normally take years to master.

A lifestyle of constant learning is Tony's goal. He not only studies more than 100 books per year, but he also has each one of them summarized so he can share the key points of the most important books with others around him. His passion to better himself links directly to his overwhelming desire to see others go further in life.

Success starts at home. Tony, his wife, and his two beautiful daughters live by a family mission that is focused on the ideals of *sharing, supporting,* and *helping others*. Tony strives to always practice what he teaches.

# TONY JEARY—MR. PRESENTATION™
# RESOURCES/PUBLICATIONS

# PRESENTATION BASICS

## Item # 1

6th Printing

### Inspire Any Audience (Hardcover)

The Ultimate Presenters Handbook

**You will learn how to:**

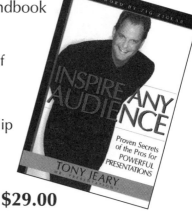

- Prepare your presentation in half the time
- Solve those "nervous jitters"
- Exceed audience expectations
- Use tools effectively including flip charts, overheads, handouts, microphones, and more . . .
- Get action from your audience

**$29.00**

## Item # 2

### Inspire Any Audience (Audio)

Proven Secrets of the Pros — Live Workshop

**You will learn:**

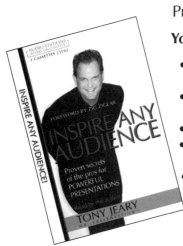

- The Seven Foundational Secrets™ that guarantee success
- Simple steps for going from nervous to natural—in seconds
- When to use humor—and when not to
- Which "little details" can make or break your presentation
- The 3-D Outline™ to save hours of preparation time

**$19.00**

Order from our website: www.MrPresentation.com

# BUSINESS RESOURCES

## Item # 3

### Strategies for Business Peak Performance

Strategy is an important factor in building a thriving organization, but few make the investment. *Strategies for Business Peak Performance* shares proven principles for business leaders to take advantage of the power of strategic planning in a fraction of time and effort commonly thought necessary.

### $29.00

## Item # 4

### Presenting Your Business Visually

From one-person businesses to multi-national corporations, branding and consistent marketing messages are critical to solid success.

**You will learn how to:**

- Fully leverage your graphic identity
- Capitalize on special event marketing
- Graphically synergize all pieces and components of a company's arsenal

### $69.00

Order from our website: www.MrPresentation.com

# TRAINING RESOURCES

## Item # 5

## The Complete Guide to Effective Facilitation
### An Instructor's Manual on Training Others

**You will learn how to:**

- Understand participant levels of behavior
- Handle difficult people and direct employees
- Form teams and implement seven ways to get involvement
- Conduct training sessions using the seven foundational secrets for facilitation
- Manipulate other logistics and support for training

**3 RING BINDER**

**$149.00**

## Item # 6

## Training Other People to Train

A "train-the-trainer" resource designed to pass along training skills to all trainers

**You will learn how to:**

- Prepare and outline your training objectives
- Set up and use your training room while utilizing training resources and presentation methods
- Know which training methods to use in which situations

**3 RING BINDER**

**$149.00**

Order from our website: www.MrPresentation.com

### Item # 7

## We've Got to Stop Meeting Like This

Simplified Meeting Management for both
Leaders and Participants

Do you believe that meetings frequently are not a good use of your time?

Do you work with people who are not sensitive to the costs related to meetings?

Have you attended a meeting recently that created more problems than it solved?

Have you ever found it hard to get a word in edgewise, or felt like putting a gag on someone who dominated a meeting?

If so, order this one simple book.

**$20.00**

### Item # 8

## The Secrets of Meeting Magic

**You will learn:**

**M**eet or not meet questions (depending on need)
**A**genda building techniques
**G**uideline ideas that will inhance all meetings
**I**nvolvement tricks
**C**larity tips in assigning and accomplishing actions and next steps

**$9.00**

### Item # 11

3 RING BINDER

## Designing Your Own Life

The Ultimate Goal Setter's Tool

This is a system Tony has used for 22 years to achieve his own personal goals

### You will learn how to:

- Clarify your mission in life
- Understand the values that drive you
- Easily organize your goals

## $99.00

### Item # 12

## Finding 100 Extra Minutes in a Day

### You will learn how to:

- **P**rioritize by becoming more proactive
- **A**void procrastination through more effective thinking
- **I**mprove your organizational skills
- **D**elegate more effectively and become more productive

3 RING BINDER **$99.00**

## Item # 13

### A Good Sense Guide to Happiness

In your business and personal life.

You'll discover encouraging and resourceful ways to maintain a healthier, happier lifestyle that will inspire you to create a more abundant and fruitful life.

A powerful collection that will guide you down the path of true success in every area of your life.

**$9.00**

## Item # 14

### Organizing Your Life

Create additional time by enhancing the accessability of things around you.

**You will learn how to:**

- Keep your tools in order, whether on the road or in the office
- Maintain an organized workspace
- Organize any closet, desk, or room to the best usage available
- Create workflows and processes that make your office a fine-oiled machine

**$29.00**

# Communication Mastery

## Item # 15

Take control of your communications.

**You will learn how to:**

- Evoke the response you want from the person with whom you are communicating
- Phrase your message in such a way to make it immediately appealing to that person
- Write correspondence or compose messages that are incredibly persuasive because they convey exactly the right message to their intended audiences

**3 RING BINDER** **$99.00**

## Item # 16

# Presenting With Style

There is a vital link between understanding personality styles and making convincing business presentations

**You will learn how to:**

- Become a convincing presenter
- Expand your paradigms to include effective use of technology
- Improve your understanding of the people to whom you will present

**$29.00**

## VIDEO WORKSHOP

### Item # 17

## Tony Jeary and Zig Ziglar

Inspire Any Audience Video

"Learn from the Pro's"
In less than 90 minutes you can gain
valuable tips from two of the best.

## 83 Minute Video Course          $95.00


Tony Jeary & Zig Ziglar
LIVE!

### Item # 18

## 6 Module Workshop

with video support, Leader's Guide
and Participant Workbook

I  What to Do before a Presentation
II  How to Effectively Prepare and
Develop a Presentation
III  Winning in the First Three Minutes
IV  The Key Skills that Make
Any Presentation Shine
V  Mastering the Tools of the Trade
VI  Summarizing and Closing
a Presentation

Call for details on licensing.
1-877-2-INSPIRE

## RECOMMENDED ASSOCIATIONS

### Meeting Professionals International (MPI)

The premier educational, technological, and networking resource in the industry. With more than 17,000 members in 64 countries with 58 chapters in 6 clubs, MPI is committed to enhancing the overall quality of meetings by ensuring the professional development and growth of its membership. International Headquarters 4455 LBJ Freeway, Suite 1200, Dallas, TX 75244 Phone: 972-702-3000 Fax: 972-702-3070

### NSA (National Speakers Association)

Association of professional speakers—individuals, some well-known authors, primarily providing keynote speeches and shorter presentations. Most cities have monthly meetings with speakers. Valuable networking, ideas, and information to shorten learning curve. National convention and regional meetings are worth attending. 3877 Seventh Street, Suite 350, Phoenix, AZ 85014. (602) 265-1001. www.speaker.org

## Toastmasters International

The world's largest organization devoted to communication excellence. Through local clubs, Toastmasters offers you the opportunity to learn effective communication through practical experience. In other words, it is a non-profit, self-supporting group of individuals who meet on a regular basis to develop basic speaking skills. Various certifications are available, guided by manuals provided by the national organization. Structure is very valuable; support is excellent. One of the best things you can do to increase your confidence in front of audiences. Very affordable. There is most likely a meeting group in your area. I attended weekly years ago—and I recommend it highly for your organization. P. O. Box 9052, Mission Viejo, CA 92690. (714) 858-8255.

## ASTD (American Society for Training and Development)

Association of trainers—mostly in-house corporate; some contract trainers and consultants. Most cities have monthly lunch or dinner meetings with speakers. Value: information, ideas, industry trends, networking contacts, annual training sessions, locally and nationally. 1630 Duke Street, P. O. Box 1443, Alexandria, VA 22313. (703) 683-8100. www.astd.org

## IABC (International Association of Business Communicators)

IABC links communicators in a global network that inspires, establishes and supports the highest professional standards of quality and innovation in organizational communication. They are recognized as the professional association of choice for communicators who aspire to excel in their chosen fields. One Hallidie Plaza, Suite 600, San Francisco, CA 94102. (415) 544-4700. www.iabc.com

# REPRODUCIBLE PAGES

# AUDIENCE WORKSHEET

What sort of knowledge about my topic do they bring to the table?

_____

_____

_____

Will they be for me or against me? Why?

_____

_____

_____

List of people whom they admire in their organization and are most likely to admire outside of it:

_____

_____

_____

Things that have worked with similar audiences in the past—and things that haven't:

_____

_____

_____

Why am I presenting?

_____

_____

_____

# 3-D OUTLINE™

Title of Presentation: _____

Objectives:

- _____
- _____
- _____

| Time | Who | What | Why | How |
|------|-----|------|-----|-----|
|      |     |      |     |     |
|      |     |      |     |     |
|      |     |      |     |     |
|      |     |      |     |     |
|      |     |      |     |     |
|      |     |      |     |     |
|      |     |      |     |     |
|      |     |      |     |     |
|      |     |      |     |     |
|      |     |      |     |     |
|      |     |      |     |     |
|      |     |      |     |     |
|      |     |      |     |     |
|      |     |      |     |     |
|      |     |      |     |     |
|      |     |      |     |     |
|      |     |      |     |     |
|      |     |      |     |     |

# BODY LANGUAGE EVALUATION

Title _____

Name of Evaluator_____

Date _____

NOTE TO THE EVALUATOR: In this presentation the speaker is concentrating on body language. He or she should use gestures, facial expressions, and other body movements that illustrate and enhance the verbal message. In evaluating this speech, focus on delivery rather than content. Use a rating scale of 1 to 10, where 1 represents unsatisfactory and 10 indicates outstanding.

| Action | Rating | Comments |
|---|---|---|
| Preparation | 1 2 3 4 5 6 7 8 9 10 | _____ |
| Organization | 1 2 3 4 5 6 7 8 9 10 | _____ |
| Appearance | 1 2 3 4 5 6 7 8 9 10 | _____ |
| Topic | 1 2 3 4 5 6 7 8 9 10 | _____ |
| Manner | 1 2 3 4 5 6 7 8 9 10 | _____ |
| Body movements | 1 2 3 4 5 6 7 8 9 10 | _____ |
| Posture | 1 2 3 4 5 6 7 8 9 10 | _____ |
| Gestures | 1 2 3 4 5 6 7 8 9 10 | _____ |
| Eye contact | 1 2 3 4 5 6 7 8 9 10 | _____ |
| Facial expressions | 1 2 3 4 5 6 7 8 9 10 | _____ |

# POST-PRESENTATION EVALUATION

Instructions: Read each group and circle the number that most closely describes how effective the presentation was in each respective area. Use a rating scale of 1 to 10 in which 1 represents unsatisfactory and 10 indicates outstanding.

Preparation and Content

| | | | | | | | | | | |
|---|---|---|---|---|---|---|---|---|---|---|
| 1. Opening | 1 | 2 | 3 | 4 | 5 | 6 | 7 | 8 | 9 | 10 |
| 2. Content material | 1 | 2 | 3 | 4 | 5 | 6 | 7 | 8 | 9 | 10 |
| 3. Organization of material | 1 | 2 | 3 | 4 | 5 | 6 | 7 | 8 | 9 | 10 |
| 4. Clarity of objectives | 1 | 2 | 3 | 4 | 5 | 6 | 7 | 8 | 9 | 10 |
| 5. Visual aids | 1 | 2 | 3 | 4 | 5 | 6 | 7 | 8 | 9 | 10 |
| 6. Handouts | 1 | 2 | 3 | 4 | 5 | 6 | 7 | 8 | 9 | 10 |
| 7. Value of exercises | 1 | 2 | 3 | 4 | 5 | 6 | 7 | 8 | 9 | 10 |
| 8. Closing | 1 | 2 | 3 | 4 | 5 | 6 | 7 | 8 | 9 | 10 |

Comments: _____

_____

Delivery

| | | | | | | | | | | |
|---|---|---|---|---|---|---|---|---|---|---|
| 1. Objectives met | 1 | 2 | 3 | 4 | 5 | 6 | 7 | 8 | 9 | 10 |
| 2. Explanation of main points | 1 | 2 | 3 | 4 | 5 | 6 | 7 | 8 | 9 | 10 |
| 3. Audience's attention | 1 | 2 | 3 | 4 | 5 | 6 | 7 | 8 | 9 | 10 |
| 4. Audience involvement | 1 | 2 | 3 | 4 | 5 | 6 | 7 | 8 | 9 | 10 |
| 5. Voice quality | 1 | 2 | 3 | 4 | 5 | 6 | 7 | 8 | 9 | 10 |
| 6. Nonverbal communication | 1 | 2 | 3 | 4 | 5 | 6 | 7 | 8 | 9 | 10 |
| 7. Questions directed to audience | 1 | 2 | 3 | 4 | 5 | 6 | 7 | 8 | 9 | 10 |
| 8. Answers to audience questions | 1 | 2 | 3 | 4 | 5 | 6 | 7 | 8 | 9 | 10 |
| 9 Time management | 1 | 2 | 3 | 4 | 5 | 6 | 7 | 8 | 9 | 10 |
| 10. Feedback | 1 | 2 | 3 | 4 | 5 | 6 | 7 | 8 | 9 | 10 |
| 11. Speaker's listening skills | 1 | 2 | 3 | 4 | 5 | 6 | 7 | 8 | 9 | 10 |
| 12. Humor | 1 | 2 | 3 | 4 | 5 | 6 | 7 | 8 | 9 | 10 |

Comments: _____

_____

Facilities

| | | | | | | | | | | |
|---|---|---|---|---|---|---|---|---|---|---|
| 1. Room | 1 | 2 | 3 | 4 | 5 | 6 | 7 | 8 | 9 | 10 |
| 2. Seating arrangement | 1 | 2 | 3 | 4 | 5 | 6 | 7 | 8 | 9 | 10 |
| 3. Acoustics | 1 | 2 | 3 | 4 | 5 | 6 | 7 | 8 | 9 | 10 |
| 4. Lighting | 1 | 2 | 3 | 4 | 5 | 6 | 7 | 8 | 9 | 10 |
| 5. Equipment | 1 | 2 | 3 | 4 | 5 | 6 | 7 | 8 | 9 | 10 |

Comments: _____

_____

# PRESENTATION ASSESSMENT

| Skill/Traits | 1 | 2 | 3 | 4 | 5 | 6 | 7 | 8 | 9 | 10 |
|---|---|---|---|---|---|---|---|---|---|---|
| **Preparation:** | | | | | | | | | | |
| Analyzing audience | — | — | — | — | — | — | — | — | — | — |
| Developing objectives | — | — | — | — | — | — | — | — | — | — |
| Developing visual aids | — | — | — | — | — | — | — | — | — | — |
| Checking logistics | — | — | — | — | — | — | — | — | — | — |
| Overcoming nervousness | — | — | — | — | — | — | — | — | — | — |
| Stating main ideas | — | — | — | — | — | — | — | — | — | — |
| Deciding supporting information | — | — | — | — | — | — | — | — | — | — |
| Creating an opener | — | — | — | — | — | — | — | — | — | — |
| Developing transitions | — | — | — | — | — | — | — | — | — | — |
| Structuring the main body | — | — | — | — | — | — | — | — | — | — |
| Using visual aids | — | — | — | — | — | — | — | — | — | — |
| Preparing the close | — | — | — | — | — | — | — | — | — | — |
| **Delivery:** | | | | | | | | | | |
| Vocal image | | | | | | | | | | |
| Volume | — | — | — | — | — | — | — | — | — | — |
| Pace | — | — | — | — | — | — | — | — | — | — |
| Pausing | — | — | — | — | — | — | — | — | — | — |
| Verbal image | | | | | | | | | | |
| Vocabulary | — | — | — | — | — | — | — | — | — | — |
| Grammar | — | — | — | — | — | — | — | — | — | — |
| Pronunciation | — | — | — | — | — | — | — | — | — | — |
| Visual image | | | | | | | | | | |
| Dress/Appearance | — | — | — | — | — | — | — | — | — | — |
| Posture | — | — | — | — | — | — | — | — | — | — |
| Gestures | — | — | — | — | — | — | — | — | — | — |
| Eye contact | — | — | — | — | — | — | — | — | — | — |
| Facial expressions/Smile | — | — | — | — | — | — | — | — | — | — |
| **Challenging situations:** | | | | | | | | | | |
| Handling questions | — | — | — | — | — | — | — | — | — | — |
| Managing mishaps | — | — | — | — | — | — | — | — | — | — |
| Controlling problem people | — | — | — | — | — | — | — | — | — | — |